T0310638

Mastering UI Mockups
and Frameworks

Mastering Computer Science
Series Editor: Sufyan bin Uzayr

For more information about this series, please visit: https://www.routledge.com/Mastering-Computer-Science/book-series/MCS

The "Mastering Computer Science" series of books are authored by the Zeba Academy team members, led by Sufyan bin Uzayr.

Zeba Academy is an EdTech venture that develops courses and content for learners primarily in STEM fields, and offers education consulting to Universities and Institutions worldwide. For more info, please visit https://zeba.academy

Mastering UI Mockups and Frameworks

A Beginner's Guide

Edited by Sufyan bin Uzayr

CRC Press
Taylor & Francis Group
Boca Raton   London   New York

CRC Press is an imprint of the
Taylor & Francis Group, an **informa** business

First edition published 2022
by CRC Press
6000 Broken Sound Parkway NW, Suite 300, Boca Raton, FL 33487-2742

and by CRC Press
4 Park Square, Milton Park, Abingdon, Oxon, OX14 4RN

CRC Press is an imprint of Taylor & Francis Group, LLC

ISBN: 9781032103167 (hbk)
ISBN: 9781032103150 (pbk)
ISBN: 9781003214748 (ebk)

DOI: 10.1201/b22860

Typeset in Minion
by KnowledgeWorks Global Ltd.

Contents

About the Editor

Sufyan bin Uzayr is a writer, coder, and entrepreneur with more than decade of experience in the industry. He has authored several books in the past, pertaining to a diverse range of topics, ranging from History to Computers/IT.

Sufyan is the Director of Parakozm, a multinational IT company specializing in EdTech solutions. He also runs Zeba Academy, an online learning and teaching vertical with a focus on STEM fields.

Sufyan specializes in a wide variety of technologies, such as JavaScript, Dart, WordPress, Drupal, Linux, and Python. He holds multiple degrees, including ones in Management, IT, Literature, and Political Science.

Sufyan is a digital nomad, dividing his time between four countries. He has lived and taught in universities and educational institutions around the globe. Sufyan takes a keen interest in technology, politics, literature, history and sports, and in his spare time, he enjoys teaching coding and English to young students.

Learn more at sufyanism.com.

CHAPTER 1

Introduction to Mockups and Wireframes

IN THIS CHAPTER

- ➤ Introduction to mockups
- ➤ Introductions to wireframes
- ➤ Basics of UI and UX

In this chapter, we'll learn about Mockups and wireframes.

Whenever we see or get interested in a website or application, we think about how it may have been designed. As we know the mentality, we'll believe that much complex software and lengthy coding have been used while constructing this thing. Most of these designs start on a simple

DOI: 10.1201/b22860-1

scale. Not every time applications and websites are made of complexities.

Whenever an application or website is designed, the designers use some techniques and tools for portraying their ideas and outlines into the product. There are three ways or levels how the designers make their contribution to the application. Here, in this article, we'll talk about the first three of them:

1. Mockups

2. Wireframes

3. Prototypes

These offer the user interface (UI) and user experience (UX) designers the opportunity to hold the rounds of user testing at each stage of their designing process. This type of testing helps the designers to check that the product they are designing is appropriate for the targeted audience, whether it meets all the expectations and how the users will navigate and draw value from the product. User testing is an essential factor here, and it should be done at the earliest if possible to avoid extra costs and efforts. These three are handy tools in the UI/UX designing process, and each one of them is an essential step for validating our ideas, checking and fixing any issues if found to minimize the budget and risk and also to save a certain amount of time, and to check what's working and what's not. A well-defined software design process lays down a visual path that you can later easily follow.

These three ways can be compared to the human body as a wireframe is a skeleton, the barebone structure of the product; Mockups can be compared to skin, facial features, hair that makes the human instantly recognizable, and the prototype are compared to the brain, the part or organ that decides how the human is interacting with others and how it should work and move. Another example we can take is that we should take these three as a map of a building. We can't start the construction of a building without having a good map for it. We have to approve the map with others and then start working and safely assume that everybody is satisfied with the overall appearance and structure so that we don't have to dismantle any part of it later. If we start the construction without the approval of stakeholders, then it will be a big problem to rebuild or dismantle it. Just like that, we can see how much effort and materials get wasted. So, using wireframes and Mockups are helpful here and make the work easier. Each of the above has different functionality and helps designers visualize and present their ideas in the product. There are some reasons why using sketches or Mockups, or wireframes are being used as we begin.

- They are being used to pitch investors, first customers and founders, and co-founders.

- They save money in the developing process, and it describes clearly what we are trying to build.

- To brainstorm or figure out what we are building. These are used to help us define our expectations.

- So let's start with the first one.

- They create the most change and impact.

- They track the progress you're making.
- They are easy for clients to understand.
- They communicate vision and expectations.
- They inform the UI.
- They allow easy collaborations.
- They are the most actionable.

Using wireframes and Mockups is perfect if we want to solve a design problem and communicate the solution. They set a vision, inspire change, and clarify understanding. And if we are creating a simple website where explaining the interactions to clients is sufficient, you likely do not need to move into the prototyping.

MOCKUPS

Mockups are the visual model of a UI. It shows how your design will appear when it is put into the real world. Mockups show typography, visuals, layouts, and the complete environment of the UI. Adobe, Sketch, and other prototyping software can be used for a Mockup. The Mockup shows how or what your final product/UI will look like. It serves as a visual draft for the same. Mockups do not serve as a live website or like that. It can be used as starting or a page, or a static button or a CTA button, as when used, it'll not open any link or window further. It may show a cover image for the product but not a catalog or link like a regular website. Mockups give users a more realistic impression of the final product.

It can be said as the face of a UI, and it shows what it will look like and doesn't tell about what or how the UI will act like. Mockups allow the designer to check how and where various elements match and work together. It reviews how a page will look like when the designer changes images, font sizes, font styles, color schemes, etc. For instance, if we use a combination of black and white for a retro website or like that, we want to check if the colors are suitable for your website. We created a Mockup and later found that the color schemes weren't ideal for our page; then, we created a second version and tested another color scheme for that.

At the starting of the process, the software analysis people understand what the user or client requires from that particular product or what is their initial needs, and by understanding that, the designing team starts working on that Mockup and then briefs the user about what/how the application will work later on. Mockups show how the UI will look and use several examples that belong to our real-life scenarios. The language used by the designing team isn't the same descriptive as used, but they use a vocabulary-free (jargon-free) language so that the user finds it easily understandable. Mockups do not always provide complete information about the final product as their visual description is not helpful in navigation and all. They show how the product will be in front of us, not how it will run.

Mockups make it easy for the designers to get their focus on the visuals of the product. As per the Mockup, it helps users/stakeholders understand the final form of the product at an early stage. These days Mockup tools are getting much attention as they help build UI specifications in companion with users.

Mockups show its uses/have advantages in many ways like:

- **Implementing Design:** As mentioned above, it makes the face of the product/UI. It gives us a good idea about what the final product will have for us. It might also provide a somewhat of how the product might function.

- **Information Architecture:** Mockups have a realistic visual appearance. They are all about organizing the product's goal and ideas and placing different elements at different positions that reveal more data and information about your product, known as "Information Architecture." Mockups are close to what the final product will be.

- **Saves Efforts:** Coding and creating a website can take loads of coding and effort. By executing and working on a Mockup, we certainly save many efforts and workloads.

- **It Helps in Maintaining Communication between the Workforce and Other Team Members:** Mockups categorize or combine people from the team that works together even when they work on other different objectives. Suppose, a team has ten members and everybody has been assigned their task. A Mockup designer can take help from or work together with a graphic designer or creative head, and who knows what they'll create or design while working together. Mockups also work as a medium of discussion between the designer and the user. The user gets the final product and gains the message that the designer and the team present in their development.

- **Immediate Valuable Feedback at Early Stages:**
  Mockups allow us to get the necessary users' feedback
  for our design. If required or found anything that isn't
  necessary or any error, it can be solved before any type
  of coding begins. We can provide our Mockups to
  several users for testing. That will help ensure that our
  product is user-friendly and works as we've made it
  to work and look like. This will save our money, time,
  and effort if we correct the mistakes or needs of our
  target audience at an early stage.

- **Translating Our Ideas into User-Friendly Language:**
  A simple grayscale and flat design will not create much
  impact in the user's mind. Users will find Mockups
  way more efficient and easy to understand about the
  product. Sometimes, it gets too difficult for the user to
  understand the idea of the product by just looking at
  a wireframe as it's just the blueprint for the product,
  and on the other hand, Mockups give a fair idea of
  how the final product will look like. This is one of the
  significant advantages of the Mockups as compared
  to wireframes.

- **Saving Money:** When designing a Mockup, we may or
  may not commit mistakes, be it more minor or significant mistakes. When we're making/creating a responsive Mockup, we at its early-stage identify problems/
  errors and correct them at that time.

We should also create our final product/UI compatible
with smaller or fewer budget devices. We should design it
that way, that it works correctly even on smaller devices.

Mockups create a layout/design that looks good and works properly even on mobile phones and desktops.

- **Easy to Understand for the User:** Mockups design or implement ideas and make the user understand the final product/result more in user-friendly language that all can understand. The other side for the Mockup is that the Framework makes it too difficult for the user to understand what the product is offering or what message is being conveyed. In that instance, Mockups has a thumbs up against Frameworks.

- **Correcting Our Mistakes More Easily:** Mockups are accessible and understandable and don't require coding and programming and all. Mockups make the product easy to recapitulate and flexible. One can correct their mistakes quickly while working with a Mockup as compared to a Framework.

Mockups, as mentioned above, have many flaws and multiple uses as compared to Frameworks. But, as we all know, the universal thing, everything has its cons as well. So let's discuss some of those here:

- **Can Become a Bloatware:** While designing a Mockup, we use several buttons here and there. The controls and options are part of the design, and before we know, we'll get bloat.

- **It Doesn't Solve Problems:** As we all know, Mockups give us an idea of what our final product will look like. It doesn't ensure us how the product will act/

work like. They serve the true purpose of any design but don't solve the problem of the users. The users shouldn't view the Mockup as isolated from the problem context. Instead, it's only the design of the final product. It does not show functionality which is the most pivotal factor while you are testing your UIs.

- **Communication Not Always Works:** Imagine, we're presenting our Mockup to an inexperienced user/stakeholder, and they have a view of it and find it excellent. Still, as we all know, Mockups are just the design, and they're just a series of isolated images. Some people might not understand the purpose of the Mockups, and they might judge the Mockup as the final product due to its appearance. That's where the communication doesn't work.

- **Confidential Issues:** When users view our Mockup, we can't limit/stop them from stealing or taking screenshots, or capturing screen recordings. We are presenting our idea in front of the users and audience with the thing in mind that they'll find our product valuable and relaxed; instead, some people can steal/copy your data, and we can't do or take any action as we haven't presented the final product. As said, Mockups are just the body, and it's a whole lot different from the final product.

- **Cost:** Mockups are expensive as we compare them to wireframes. If we are building the basic structure for our product and are low on funds/finance, we can use wireframes instead of Mockups to save money. Making Mockup designs can become a slight load on the pocket as we compare them to the cost of creating wireframes.

- **A Bit Time-Consuming:** As we all know, Mockups are the design for our product. We design the Mockups and show the users how our final product will look like. First of all, we create our ideas and designs. Then we place or categorize every element in our development. All this takes time, and who knows, the method we're creating for our product comes out in a different product before launching our final product. Some ideas are shared, and if we can use them in our Mockups, why can't others use them too?

There is another type of Mockup, or we can say better Mockups. We can define them as high-fidelity Mockups. There is a lack of interactions in Mockups, as we know. In some cases, we want the user to be able to interact between different elements. For that con of Mockups, we can use high-fidelity Mockups. These Mockups work as if it is an actual website or a mobile application to interact and react. These kinds of Mockups include some crucial interactions that the final product will have.

As we know, they are better Mockups, and they'll definitely require more time, and also, it will bring up the costs of product development. The time needed to create a high-fidelity Mockup will be more than developing essential Mockups. But, if we invest time in high-fidelity Mockups, it will give us something. The time invested in these Mockups will point out flaws in our Mockup, and we can fix those flaws before those flaws become more costly and stressful. The design for high-fidelity Mockups is also time-consuming, but those interactions made won't just be thrown away. Following are some advantages of using high-fidelity Mockups:

1. It eases and increases communication and understanding between the user and other team members too.

2. It reduces the risk of further upgrading and modification of requirements by the users.

3. Speeds up exploring end-to-end conceptual design.

4. Up for using high-fidelity Mockups is the illuminating effect on your navigation flow (it's a complex aspect of UX design that no designer can afford to not test at an early stage).

Creating these type of Mockups and other Mockups too require user involvement. User is the essential thing kept in mind while framing these. Users should be asked and questioned about the needs and requirements they're fulfilling through our product. Polls should be created for that, and their feedback should be welcomed, heard, and implemented.

Different Components of a Mockup

As we all know, Mockups are advanced wireframe versions. The difference is that a Mockup shows what the final product will look like. The users get a fair idea of how the last website or mobile application will be like, how it will shape up, and how and where various components will look and be placed. A complete Mockup requires different parts like:

1. The colors and graphics will be seen in the complete and final version of the product.

2. The content layout.

3. Navigation graphics (buttons and text).

4. Typography as per the design of the product.

5. Buttons, text bars, and other visual arts.

Sometimes a question arises that whether Mockups are dynamic or static? As per the information say they are fixed. And we know that Mockups give us a view of how the final product will be after completion. When we compare Mockups to wireframes and prototypes, Mockups are more efficient because it takes a shorter time instead of drawing one. They are much easier for planning out how the final product will look like. The designers' team designs wireframes, and later on, these wireframes become proper Mockups.

Creating and Designing

We can design Mockups through various applications available like Adobe and all. We have to build and create the Mockup keeping our target audience in mind. There's no point in designing a Mockup if it's not going to be for anyone. Our Mockup should be clickable and should navigate to other pages properly. Having a clickable Mockup has many advantages as we know having something that users can navigate and click on brings much feedback regarding all the aspects of our Mockup. So let's start with how we can design a good and proper Mockup step-by-step.

- **Graphic Designing:** The designing elements and the navigation elements too have to be straightforward to understand. They should be text-aligned, and font styles should be set accordingly. Different buttons should be given different sizes, font styles, and how they're going to work.

  Keep color scheme in mind. Colors should be selected according to the plan that provides a good UI that matches other colors and should make your UI more different and attractive. Getting wrong color schemes can lead to the downfall of our product very quickly. As a user sees your product, he makes up his mind that the colors are not matching; sometimes, the colors for different buttons get inverted, which further makes everything messed up and doesn't look good.

  Also, proper images related to your content should be used – good quality images and graphics for better results. Designers should use suitable UI kits to make users understand well, as they should be familiar with the design and language you're using.

  Another thing to keep in mind is the typography. Using proper typography gains users to focus and improve the overall appearance. A good hierarchy should be followed for the elements and text in the UI. Too large fonts or too small fonts shouldn't be used as they will spoil the overall look and appearance of the UI. Also, too many fonts shouldn't be used. Using two to three fonts is okay as too many fonts can clash, and it won't give an excellent experience to the user. Italics and Bold texts should be used according to the needs as well as font size too.

The content in our Mockup shouldn't be too much, and it shouldn't be too less too. Using good texting and proper images will generally make up the user's mind of the right and final product.

Some navigation and buttons should be used. Our Mockup should be navigable and clickable as it will lead to more effectiveness at communicating our ideas to the users. Enough interactive elements should be used to explore the Mockup from one page to another easily.

In our Mockup, we should combine our pages by hierarchy. The pages should be in order from start to end.

- **User Research:** Identifying users and their needs is a central aspect of the Mockup. We need to ensure that our users know what a Mockup is, what functions it serves, and how it differs from the final product. When with the created Mockup, we have the idea about the main objective of our website; one thing we have to know is there is a need for the website. If the users understand and view your Mockup and decide that they need something else, then our idea can sink and fail. That's why online surveys have to be conducted to identify our users and user needs. We have to understand and identify the group of people/target audience who are keenly interested in our website/

product before working on our Mockup. We can get this user-related information from different surveys, questionnaires, etc.

- **User Testing:** When the visual, essential elements and layouts are completed, we must start testing the users. We can begin user testing, and for that, there are three categories.

  1. **Explorative:** It is the first and earliest step to check the usability and effectiveness of the created Mockup.

  2. **Assessment:** It is the midway step for the checking, and it is used for checking product development and overall usability test related to technology. It contains whether the technology used in our Mockup determines satisfaction, general usability, and effectiveness.

  3. **Comparative:** In this step, we compare our technology used and design with other similar products and check the strengths and weaknesses of both.

- **Correcting Errors and Applying Necessary Changes:** When we arrive at this step, we must check problems and errors, if any. Often this step needs to be repeated several times. Then after we cross-checked it several times, we should ask the user for their feedback and make the rectifications wherever necessary. We should try to fix the mistakes as early as possible to save money.

- **Final Development:** After making a proper and correct Mockup for the product, it is handed over to the development team, and following that, the team starts to work on it and other code of the product. We should help the developing section by providing documentation like user flows, requirements of the users, stylesheets, etc.

Some Tools Used to Create Mockups

1. **Figma:** Figma is a design tool that works directly on your browser. It is a web-based graphics editing and UI design application that can do all kinds of graphic and designing work like framing wireframes and Mockups, prototyping designs, modifying mobile app interfaces, etc. One key advantage of using Figma is that you can start creating from any desktop or other platform without purchasing installation software or additional licenses.

   Figma runs on any operating system with a web browser in it, be it Macs, Windows PC, and all. By using Figma, one can check in to see what the team is designing in real-time. Another significant advantage of using Figma for building Mockups is memory management. It manages all the assets appropriately, and one can easily have all project assets in one single file with multiple pages, and it also loads instantly. It is easily accessible and keeps everything on one page, which gives Figma a great up against its competitors.

2. **Mockplus:** It is a cloud-based tool that is used for making Mockups. It's a simple tool that helps designers with limited experience create Mockups effectively and efficiently. They don't require to learn huge

coding for making Mockups here. It offers online collaboration that allows users to work with their team members, compare the designs, test designs differently, etc. Users can also give their feedback here by commenting there. It also allows users to finish the design fast. Instead of overemphasizing functionalities, this agile tool provides the user with experience the highest priority. It's a highly intuitive interface, and user-centric interaction has gained many customers globally. It not only lets designers quickly make practical and interactive Mockups, but it also offers a fluid view of Mockups on any device, be it a mobile or a desktop. Now, both IOS and Android have the Mockplus application available.

WIREFRAMES

It is another way less complex than the Mockups. It is used to design websites/UI at a primary and structural level. It is a blueprint for a website. For example, an architect shows the basic blueprint of what they plan to build as the final product. Similarly, in website/UI designing, a blueprint is made referring to as a wireframe. It is an essential step that shows where images, videos, and elements will appear in our final product. They are generally part of the software.

Wireframes are different from the Mockups but provide the same function. The Mockup shows the complete design, fonts used, navigation buttons, good imaging, etc. But when we see a wireframe, it offers a basic idea of how the website will look.

Wireframes specify which interface elements will be there on essential pages, which is vital for designing.

Wireframes provide the user with an early-stage idea of what the final product will look like. By understanding the wireframes of a product, users and stakeholders learn about that wireframe and approve the team to start the creative phase of building the application.

Using wireframes gives quicker and cheaper results and amends the structure of the critical pages in a format. The development of the wireframes to the final stage will provide the users and the design team the idea that the page is keeping in mind the user needs as it's essential and completing project objectives.

We can draw a wireframe with our bare hands. But for proper functioning and understanding, they're put in collaboration with software like Sketch, Microsoft Visio, etc. In some cases, when the wireframes are going to be used for a prototype, HTML is also used.

Why Should We Wireframe

- **Hold a Demo for Clients:** Getting feedback from users/stakeholders is a critical component of the designing process. We can present a demo or blueprint in front of the users to give a rough idea of how the product will be. Although Mockups provide more light to the final product's appearance, wireframes perform how a blueprint works. If users find something irrelevant or not up to their mark, we can face multiple change requests from our users, which is normal. Using wireframes, we can do this task very effectively and efficiently. Making changes to a Mockup requires more time and cost as compared to the wireframes.

- **Help the Team Estimate the Work and Scope of Work:** By creating wireframes, designers quickly represent the future product and demonstrate it to the team to get their feedback and ideas. Also, wireframes allow us to involve developers in discussing designs at early stages, enabling them to give necessary feedback and suggest changes before the visual designing starts. Looking through a wireframe is way faster than reading specifications. It also helps us show to our team which elements and controls will be seen on the pages, how the components will interact, and avoid discrepancies in scope between the initial estimates and the final ones.

- **Carrying Out User Testing:** Rolling out a website/application without the users knowing how to use that product is of no use. Wireframes can help designers get valuable and necessary feedback from the users/stakeholders.

Quintessential Points to Have in Mind for Creating Better Wireframes for Better Results

- **Minimize the Colors:** As we know, the use of wireframes, adding colors to a wireframe might distract the user's attention and make any other updates more difficult. Also, if a user doesn't know what wireframes or Mockups are and what they perform, they might judge a colored wireframe as a final design. The important and the only goal of a wireframe is to show which elements the product will have and how they should interact with each other. This doesn't mean that colors are prohibited while working on wireframes.

Sometimes using colors to highlight specific components is okay.

- **Use Real Content:** Using accurate content in a wireframe is crucial to keep in mind. We have often seen that the UI/UX designers don't add actual content in the wireframes and often use "Lorem Ipsum" instead. Using this won't let you see the whole picture and will likely need to make any adjustments or corrections to the UI. Using accurate content will add value to the wireframe created and indicate that we need to gather the actual content. Also, it will explain the context better

- **Using Annotations:** If some design solutions can't be illustrated by viewing, that's why the users or even the developers can have some doubts relating that. In that case, on-screen annotations can be provided to explain the logic behind them.

- **Low–High Fidelity:** So basically, there are three types of wireframes that we'll discuss in the next topic. Some projects may require a low fidelity and a basic wireframe. In contrast, some projects require high-fidelity advanced wireframes, and choosing a wireframe depends on what product/website/application you are building. We should not hesitate to use low or high wireframes according to the need, as adding more details and information to your wireframe won't be a problem for the developers. If the team is very short of time or funds, they can go for the low-fidelity wireframes, but high-fidelity wireframes are the go if you have ample time and proper funding.

- **Maintaining Consistency:** Showing consistency is a crucial aspect of wireframes, and it reduces the chances of confusion. Same or similar components should look the same on all our wireframes. If they look different, the developers are likely to question if they are actually the same and sometimes add extra time to the estimates because the designs are different.

- **Simple Designing for the Components:** Basic designs should be used when adding features to our wireframes. As we know, wireframes don't contain appropriately designed and complex ingredients. Instead of them, parts should be designed so that they should be easily recognizable by our team members and other users/ stakeholders. Adding intricate details will increase the amount of time taken, and also it can increase the cost of making the wireframe.

Different Types of Wireframes

There are three common types of wireframes:

1. **Low-Fidelity Wireframe:** The wireframes that are created as paper wireframes and are created roughly come under this category of wireframes. It typically starts as a simple static outline on paper or digital canvas. These are quick outlines and are easy to revise and construct. Also, they do not focus on scales, grids, or pixels either they focus on functions, headings, topics, contents and present them in a raw form without an accurate structure. They are concerned with the user flow. Other detailing like color and graphics are not the primary goal for this type of wireframe.

When we have many wireframes to create, we need to work quickly to keep our projects moving along. We can make these wireframes anytime, wherever, or whenever our mind strikes with an idea relating to our product. They are easily adjustable as they are rough sketches. Some standard tools for creating this type of wireframe are *Balsamiq* and Sketch.

Also, they are used to outline visual and typographic hierarchies, transitions, navigations, and interactions.

These wireframes can support brainstorming sessions at different stages of development. They are good to use when you want input and feedback from multiple users/stakeholders. As we know, these are used at the early stages of development; we can go back to the drawing board whenever we need.

These low-fidelity wireframes have some critical benefits for early design planning. Let's discuss some of them:

- **Less Time-Consuming:** A low-fidelity wireframe can be constructed in minutes and completed in one team sitting. This allows sketching out and comparing multiple ideas fast. These wireframes are the outlines. Simple text and placeholders can be used in these wireframes to communicate our ideas effectively and quickly.

- **Collaborative:** These type of wireframes doesn't require unique designing or coding skills. So we can get ideas and inputs from other team members too. The people from technical backgrounds help, but other people and team members can help you too.

- **Inexpensive:** While constructing these, all we require is a pen and paper or using a digital canvas. Here, we are creating a simple outline, and there is no need for using huge funds and additional costs into the development.

2. **Mid-Fidelity Wireframe:** Unlike the lower ones, they contain grids, scales, pixels, and therefore, they are much more accurate than the lower ones. They are commonly used for communication with the end users and the stakeholders. They are the most common form of wireframes used these days by designers. They start to define various UI elements with a focus on functionality. Using these types of wireframes is a good choice if we're creating a wireframe map or working through multiple design steps before designing a fully functional prototype. A wireframe map has combined various wireframes functioning for each page. They are created to become comprehensive roadmaps for the development process. Here, we need to make quite a good number of wireframes, and here, low-fidelity wireframes won't work as they would not provide much detail and clarity. It is advised to create medium-fidelity wireframes as they do not take a considerable amount of time. It is easily understandable when others are following the wireframe map later on. If our project has enough budget and time, the mid-fidelity wireframes are the succession after the low fidelity. There is no problem if

we add some further details and development to our design ideas.

They are usually shown as Black & White digital, or they can be hand-drawn sketches too. The content layout and the complete structure here are somewhat clearly defined, excluding the graphics and design.

3. **High-Fidelity Wireframe:** This type of wireframe is the most advanced type of wireframe, and they contain colors, images, graphics, and written content. This type of wireframe has the complete blueprint of the design and is the most accurate one. They show more detail and higher-level renderings for each element. Their deep focus is on the content layout. They closely resemble the final product and are created digitally. They are best applied after an initial brainstorming session when we've already mapped out the basic structure of the application. They are the succession of a design based on a low-fidelity wireframe. They should be reserved for projects that have been approved by the users/stakeholders and are cleared for production. These wireframes make it easy to communicate the various qualities of the product we are creating. They also tend to consume more designing time, and definitely, they will be more expensive to construct. Creating high-fidelity wireframes should not be an issue if we have the approvals necessary to move forward and a reasonable budget.

They are used to present a simple but realistic idea of what and how the final interface/final product will be like. This type of wireframe helps the team and the users make more informed decisions about what elements are missing, what factors are working or not working, what usability issues can exist before they invest more time. These can be made using tools like InVision.

High-fidelity wireframes are advised to use when you have:

- **Time:** These types of wireframes are worth the time because they help you make a better final product. These ensure that you get everything you want without too many successions to the design once it starts production. If you get to a high-fidelity wireframe, typically, it means you've received input from various users with varying expertise. These types of wireframes are not advisable when we are working on a short timeline or shorter budget.

- **A Personal Project:** If we are working on a personal project, high-fidelity wireframes are recommended to convince someone else to give us funds for moving forward in the development process. High-fidelity wireframes are more than just a basic wireframe, and it attracts interest from investors; for this, we need a visual that can fully illustrate our product's potential.

Just like Mockups, wireframes also have their uses/advantages too. Let's discuss some of them:

1. **Improving Efficiency and Collaborations:** The developers build the standard and basic structure and then recheck their designs. If the team find some errors may it be small or bigger ones, they realize sooner or

at the early stages that something isn't working and thus find a solution and get it fixed. This requires proper and robust wireframes.

These proper wireframes allow the development team, designing team, and content creation team to work together to develop the product and give everyone involved a base in starting from. With that, everyone can work on their work and influence what other team members are doing simultaneously. It can reduce the communication barrier between you and your team members. Sometimes, it is also an excellent way to demonstrate your design ideas to customers and other users, and stakeholders.

2. **Organizing Information with Wireframes:** Using proper and well-made wireframes, hierarchy, flow, structure, and relationships between content and the pages can be quickly determined. After creating the wireframe, we get to see the information into a visual layout and see how or where several elements and items will be structured and connected. Hence, making it easier to spot any apparent gap if found.

3. **Fostering Client Development:** After viewing and understanding the wireframe, the user can separate the functionality and layout of the wireframe. It allows them to focus on the bones of the website first. Before the users get involved in the overall looking and appearance of the website, they can firstly provide feedback on how they want the website to function. After functionality, users can review the pages with creative appearances and designs to see the

visual aspects. Wireframing allows us to understand how certain features will function and see the relationship between screens.

4. **Pushing Usability to the Front:** This is a crucial advantage of using a wireframe. Usability is an essential requirement of the design. In wireframes, the usability is pushed to the front showing the page layouts. Before the graphics, appearances, and images, it focuses on the website's bones that make the users look at the website's navigations, ease of use, naming and placing of links, feature placement, etc.

5. **Saves Time and Effort:** As wireframes are the blueprints, they save time in many ways. Unlike the designs, the development team finds wireframes easy to understand and easy to construct while keeping the blueprint in mind. It also eases communication between the crew and also avoids misunderstandings. Everyone from the development team, the designing team, and the user gets on the same page and solves the task of what the interface is, what it's supposed to do, and how it will function.

6. **Making Content Development Effective:** Wireframes make content development easy and understandable. Either the search engine or the human eye will find the undifferentiated text hard to read and understand. Large blocks of text shouldn't be used. Both SEO and human eyes prefer elegant content to the bigger heavy ones. With the wireframes, we can overview the contents. We can check the font styles, arrange fonts, use bullets and heads properly, etc.

7. **Makes the Design Process Stepwise:** All the critical elements for the website shouldn't be combined and done simultaneously. Every step of every component should be done step-by-step. Wireframes ensure that all these steps are taken one at a time. This indeed allows the team members and the users too to give feedback at an early stage. If we don't use wireframes and delay the input, it increases the cost for correcting it, and without wireframes, completed Mockups have to be corrected, and it takes much time, money, and effort.

8. **Core Message:** Wireframes help deliver the core message/purpose of our website more effectively and appropriately and help gather feedback early.

9. **Low Cost:** If we think practically, the cost of creating a wireframe with a pen and paper is "ZERO." If we are trying to make wireframe with a wireframing tool, even that cost is meager. Using wireframes is a perfect option for you and your team to visualize the macro aspects and decide on the design directions of the website.

   Making a proper wireframe is essential. It can have its problems too if it's not completed correctly. Let's discuss how to make an excellent and successful wireframe.

   • **Using the Correct Amount of Detailing:** Too much detailing shouldn't be used at the beginning. We can add more details to our wireframe to show it to the user and our team too. As we all know, wireframes are blueprints and can be drawn on paper too, and Rough sketches allow us to come up with new ideas and more solutions for the users. A wireframe should be practical and essential, and we should make something that others can collaborate around.

- **Color and Design:** As we start with the primary constructing of a wireframe, we should try to work in grayscale as it helps maintain focus on the primary function of the process. Wireframes are made to decide the layout and location of the elements of the website. They finalize the form, not the design.

- **Use Grids if Necessary:** The elements we are placing in the layout must be adjustable, scalable, and interchangeable. Using grids can help different layout parts to their position. Using grids is a way to construct our wireframe faster.

- **Using Colors Somewhere if Necessary:** Colors give an excellent and aesthetic look, and it directs the user's eye to the essential elements. As we've discussed that wireframes are the basic blueprints, colors aren't advised to be used in them. But we can use some; it's not that colors aren't allowed or something like that. We can change user colors somewhere and should use them consistently. We can use color to highlight some critical topic or object. Too many colors should not be used as colors can be distracting.

- **Use Notes/Comments/Footnotes:** As we know, wireframes are blueprints, and maybe somewhere, it's easy for the developers to understand, but the users find it hard to read and understand. Some brief annotations or notes can be used. The main purpose is to make it easier for the users to understand the meaning and purpose of our design. It also helps to create context.

- **Demand Feedback:** After constructing a proper wireframe, we should share our ideas with the users and other people to get their opinions on our work. Getting feedback early is good as if a user isn't satisfied with something or there's an error, we can rectify it early on and save money and time.

While we talked about the pros of using wireframes and how to create proper wireframes, now we should also learn about some of the cons that wireframes have.

1. **Designing of the Wireframe:** As we know, they are the blueprints; using too much design here is unnecessary as they serve to map out the fundamental flow and a basic version of our website. Too much designing there is not required, and it also kills much time.

2. **Sometimes Act Like an Extra Step in the Process:** Many believe and claim that skipping the wireframing step is not a problem, and cutting it will get things moving onto the designing team faster.

3. **Client Satisfaction:** As we know, we live in a vast world, and everyone here has different thinking toward the website/product we are designing. More clients these days are concerned more with how a website looks

than how it works. Clients get more interested and comfortable looking at the graphics, images, and of course, branding. They won't show much interest in a gray, basic map or blueprint of the website.

While we talked about the ups and downs of the wireframes, some people claim that the wireframing process can be removed, and the design process should work without wireframes. People claim that Mockups are much easier for maintenance. Let's discuss some points that say skipping wireframe is okay.

- **Brainstorming:** The developers at the early stage should make quick paper sketches and present them to the team and users, too, if possible, and discuss with them. Sketching the ideas seems to be better and effective. Drawings will give a fair idea about your product too.

- **Analysis:** We should learn about what the user needs from our product. We should discover the requirements they are trying to fulfill through our development and initial researches. We can make notes about what/how the users require and all. Making paper notes make it more effective for our brain to keep those critical things in mind while working.

- **Unleashing More Creativity:** As discussed, sketches, sketching, and writing on paper unleash our potential. While sketching or drawing on paper, we try to be more focused and creative while working on a wireframe. This will give better results.

- **Proper Understanding of the Idea:** Sketches are simple to make, and everyone understands them well. We discussed that wireframes are blueprints. Not everyone understands that their requirements are fulfilled for the product while viewing just a wireframe. Sketches or high-fidelity Mockups provide a fair idea of what the final product will be in front of the clients.

- **Fitting in the Modern World:** As we know, the world has developed a lot in the field of technology, and with that, one thing is clear that the modern, efficient design workflow is the one without wireframes. They were influential in the past when there were no or not many practical digital tools. Now, when we have the technology, why settle for less?

- **Get Feedback:** Final sketches should be prepared and discussed with the team, and if the client is present, we can discuss those with him too and get their feedback before doing the high-fidelity work.

Some other alternatives can be used in place of using wireframes. The main objective behind skipping wireframes is efficiency.

1. **Sketches (UI Sketching):** By using drawings against wireframes, we can get fast and correct results at almost the same value as wireframes. Sketching is a thumbs up if we are comparing it to wireframes.

2. **High-Fidelity Mockups:** Many excellent and modern tools are flowing in the market for designing in the current technology. Many designing tools like Adobe, Mockplus, Moqups are used to create these high-end Mockups. With these tools, we are jumping right into high-fidelity Mockups after sketching is possible effectively.

For more significant types of websites and applications, it is a crucial step to have a wireframe. Some sites need wireframes, with the first few frames aiding other builds. Wireframes are helpful in mainly web-based applications such as mobile applications, portal systems, etc. So to conclude, what are wireframes is an essential and initial part of the project as they build the blocks to great user-centered design, ensure proper navigation, and allow the perfect layout of the critical pages. It also provides the designing team and the other crew with the confidence of what is being created for the client. Wireframes will help save time and somewhat cost as if we are testing and amending changes in the later designing process, and it will cost us more if we rectify them at the wireframing stage only.

Some Wireframing Tools

- **A Pen and Paper:** Using a pen and paper is an easy way to start building a wireframe. Sketching (be it rough or fair) is a good and efficient way of getting ideas transferred from our brain into the world so that we can revise, revisit the concepts, and review them. No matter if we make a mistake while drawing them as they can be thrown or replaced or re-drawn at any moment.

- **Freehand, InVision:** It is a digital whiteboard where our team and we can communicate and collaborate to share ideas and get reviews. The wireframes that are created in Freehand can be shared and be collaborative. Uploading our hand-drawn wireframes and saving tedious steps of scanning is easily possible with the help of Freehand. Freehand gives everyone on the team the power to share their idea in a way that makes sense to everyone, whether that's a rough or fair sketch or drawing or dropping ideas, images, and inspirations. Anyone that is only there for giving feedback can also be there with the team on Freehand. Freehand can be accessed on any new-age electronic device – iPad, Tablet, Laptop, and Mobile Phone. Freehand allows us to do many things that are necessary while building up a wireframe:

1. Save and share our work.

2. Re-draw sketches and share rough ideas with others.

3. Add artboards or images from other applications.

4. Zoom in and out.

5. Undo, redo, and scaling too.

6. Provide feedback to the team.

- **Wirify, Volkside:** It is a modern-day tool that lets you turn any webpage into a wireframe in just one click. It is used for analyzing pages in a transparent and efficient, and streamlined way. They are less used for just creating wireframes. It's lightweight and works in almost every modern-day browser.

- **Axure RP:** Axure is one of the best tools used for UI and UX designing. Axure RP generates HTML websites for preview and team collaboration too. We can easily simulate animations and transitions right within the tool. We can also create wireframes, flow diagrams, data flows, and many more with the help of Axure. We can easily create visual styles and reusable UI patterns that can be accessed across the entire organization. Also, we can easily share our wireframes and documentation via password-protected links and create a workspace to communicate and collaborate with other team members. Working together on the same project is very efficient on this platform. We can work together from the next desk or any other corner of the world. Low-fidelity wireframes can easily be converted into high-fidelity wireframes for realistic usability testing and developer handoff.

- **Pencil:** This software provides rich shapes and diagrams that help present our design ideas roughly and fairly side-by-side and build efficient website wireframes. It is a free-to-access and open-source tool.

- **Wireframe CC:** It is one of the essential tools available for creating wireframes. It is a simple designing tool that helps us make wireframes with essential and straightforward elements like squares, circles, boxes, images, etc. It allows us to access wireframes anywhere and anytime and lets us export our wireframes and other projects to PDF files for further succession.

DIFFERENCES BETWEEN MOCKUPS AND WIREFRAMES

Mockups and wireframes serve differently while using them in the designing process. Let's talk about some differences between Mockups and wireframes.

1. Wireframes are basic, black and white renderings and are the blueprints of the final product. They focus on what the outcome will do. They are just a scheme of our product's UI and don't have any visual design elements; Mockups are static yet realistic renderings of what or how the product will look like. It provides the early appearance of how the final product will be. Mockups are the next step as we add visuals and use graphics and design elements like color, font, images, style, etc.

2. When we see the cost of constructing these two, wireframes cost much less as compared to Mockups. Wireframes, as we know, are basic sketches that are hand-drawn, and these require no cost at all. Wireframing tools also charge very little and too little when we compare them to the tools we use to build Mockups. While we know, Mockups are made with the help of tools like Sketch, Figma, InVision, and many more. These tools cost more than the wireframing tools.

3. The goal of a Mockup is to present as close as possible what the final product will be in front of us and how all last appearances will be rendered. On the other hand, the goal of a wireframe is to fit the elements into a proper layout. They don't indicate how details

may appear in a final design. Wireframes are never called a Mockup, but in some cases, Mockups can be used as wireframes, but this would have implications for any required revisions and significantly impact the company's budget.

4. The wireframes do not have specific colors or fonts as they are just the design's basic and static draft layouts. It is easy to make an initial draft to bring clarity on what is required. Comparing it to Mockups is also a fixed page layout, but it showcases how the final product will look. It is an exact representation of how the web page/final product will look like.

5. Wireframes help us to clarify our projects and give us an overall understanding of the UI. Also, they let us define project goals and priorities and make it easier to communicate our ideas to the design team. Whereas, Mockups help us to understand what our product will look like in the visual areas. It's a perfect transition from wireframes, and you don't have to rely on your imagination solely to understand the graphic and visual design of our product. It helps us reflect our vision of the product's design and decide what changes we'd like to make or what things we have to correct.

CHAPTER 2

Mockup Tools

IN THIS CHAPTER

➤ Adobe XD

➤ Mockplus

➤ Moqups

➤ Mockplus iDoc

We have discussed Mockups and Wireframe in the previous chapter, and now we will discuss different kinds of Mockups in this chapter. It is a fact that creating a Mockup is an unavoidable part of designing a website or application. Anyhow, the web design workflow can always intimidate anyone who isn't that trained in designing or product managing. To add to the confusion, different steps in the design process are often perplexed for each other or sometimes are mischaracterized.

DOI: 10.1201/b22860-2

Eventually, this unique guide will let you understand precisely what a Mockup is, where it can be put in the design process, how it can be used, and those who are required to be well versed more than the very tenet of a Mockup.

INTRODUCTION

What Is a Mockup?

A Mockup is a static web page or application design that attributes many of its final design components, but it may not be functional. A Mockup is not precisely decorated as a live page and usually contains some placeholder data.

It's important to elaborate here on that definition.

As a "static design," the functionality of a live website is not included in a Mockup. Even though a Mockup would contain a colored CTA button, as an example, it would not pop up a form when clicked on, unlike a website or the prototype of a website. A Mockup may sometimes light up a cover image at the top of the page, but it is unlikely to have an active carousel like a website.

You might have known that a Mockup is not the first stage of website development, so it's on its way to being a completed product, but it still has a ways to go. A Mockup may contain placeholder copy or images, but it is meant to provide an excellent feeling of the page, though not what it will act like.

What Is the Purpose of Mockups?

It serves as a visual draft of a web application or page. It is developed to bring life to an idea or Wireframe and let a designer examine how different visual elements work together.

Mockups allow stakeholders to examine what that page will look like while suggesting appropriate changes in color, images, style, layout, and more. If you are curious about a page using a secondary color, you can examine how that will pop up by creating a second version of the Mockup. Likewise, if you need to make any kind of change, like inserting a header while centering an image, your Mockup can allow the team to watch how that specific change might look.

A page needs to be created for a particular purpose with a determined goal in mind. Mockups allow the team to see how that purpose can be attained through the layout developed by a user interface (UI) designer with a Wireframe and how that layout can become a reality using their visual creativity and brand standard.

Where Do Mockups Come into the Web Design Process?

When we consider stages, Mockups come at approximately the midpoint of the web design process, and when it comes to time, they're still in the early stages of design.

A simple design process looks like this:

- Ideation.
- Wireframing.
- Mockup.
- Prototyping.
- Go live.

The wireframing stage is about creating a rough layout for the page, taking a goal or an idea, and using design theory to create a page that will achieve that goal. The Mockup is often used to take that layout and make it more flexible and lifelike.

After stakeholders reach an agreement on the visual aspects of the Mockup, it goes into the prototyping stage, where actual development is required to turn a Mockup into an almost near-functional version of the page. Indeed, all of this happens before a page goes live and is tested with real users or visitors.

What Is the Distinction between a Wireframe and Mockup?

A Mockup comes to post a Wireframe in the design process, and it builds upon the design of the Wireframe. Mockups certainly are more robust and closer to a fine product than a Wireframe.

There is some kind of differences that can offer you keep Wireframes and Mockups straight:

- Wireframes are black and white, but Mockups are in color.

- When Wireframes are used for functionality, Mockups are used for visuals.

- Wireframes exhibit simply elements of a page; Mockups give substance.

An analogy for both is like the Wireframe represents the blueprint of a house. In two dimensions and black and white, it exhibits the house's layout and how the rooms interconnect.

If a Wireframe is a blueprint, then a Mockup is a two-dimensional rendering of a standing home. It exhibits the style of trim and color of the siding. It provides a cross-section of the living room, finished with wallpaper and granite for the fireplace.

These images can speedily be altered to show different types of wallpaper or a darker wood floor. In the same way, a Mockup can manifest stakeholders' variety of visual looks to a page without altering its structure.

Mockup and a Prototype?

Mockups always come before prototypes, which are a semblance of what a live page will be. Mockup is a static image; a prototype provides most of the functionality of a live website, providing stakeholders something very near to the actual user experience (UX).

If we go to the architectural comparison, imagine that a Mockup is an image created on a computer screen or easel; the prototype is a three-dimensional virtual reality program that allows you to walk through the home. The image will enable you to see the way colors work collectively or the layout of a single room; the computer program would allow you to simulate walking from one particular room to the nearest one to experience the open floor plan or get an idea of how tight a hallway feels.

In the same way, a prototype allows stakeholders to put themselves in the shoes of a genuine user and provide them almost next to an authentic experience as possible before pushing a page live.

For Creating Mockups

To get an idea of what a Mockup is and what it's used for is one thing. It's a whole other attempt to create a Mockup that is helpful in the development process.

As a beginner, you have got to use software of some kind to create the Mockup. What type and product will differ based on what tools you used, your budget, who else is required to access the Mockup, and more.

There are particular wireframing tools, and some of these tools also provide the capability to create Mockups, even though, generally speaking, it's standard to use two separate devices.

Another option possible is to use a general graphic design tool to build Mockups. Adobe Illustrator is generally the tool you have got to use to create them. This kind of vector design product is the industry standard for all sorts of designers, and it has been widely used to generate more than a fair share of Mockups. Its widespread presence in the industry gives many tutorials, templates, and more for the inexperienced designer.

Finally, there are tools designed particularly for creating Mockups. Some products are mainly marketed towards the Mockup stage, but this software category is mysterious to an extent. Products are always marketed for either Mockups and Wireframes or Mockups and prototypes. Choosing a product can be challenging, but using a software review site or getting recommendations from fellow designers can let you navigate this software space.

MOCKUP TOOLS

A Mockup is a kind of visual presentation of a website or app. Designers always use Mockups to project their website's layout and functionality to their prospective clients.

While Wireframes and prototypes are low-fidelity formats, Mockups are more intuitive. They help clients visualize how the final product will look, feel, and work.

Mockups also help remove ambiguity regarding the client's expectations. Clients can detect gaps on the website by looking at its Mockup and suggesting early product revisions. By using Mockups for each iteration, designers can create a final product that meets client requirements.

This means a Mockup can make or break your website.

In this guide, we will talk about websites and tools to generate brilliant Mockups.

A. ADOBE XD

Adobe XD is a vector-based UI and UX design tool, and it is possible to design anything from smartphone apps to full-blown websites. Let's now look at what it offers designers and why it's become such a powerful tool in the web design industry. Adobe XD was first launched as "Project Comet" back in 2015 at the annual Adobe MAX conference. Back then, it provided a breath of fresh air to anyone still using Photoshop or Illustrator for their same UI design. Not only that, the web introduces very different design challenges to print.

Adobe XD is a popular UI and UX tool.

Those who started out designing websites in Photoshop are aware of the struggles, importantly were responsive and fluid design is considered. But XD is an entirely different thing. It was created from the ground up, especially with UI and UX design in its mind, so obviously, it has several features which never available in other graphics applications.

One of the significant contentions often faced by an industry giant like Adobe is a dinosaur with less capacity to be as competent as its younger competitors. Anyhow, a company like Adobe has the resources to evolve and grow spectacularly and the financial stability that would eventually make mastering Adobe XD a good investment. This is what makes it a huge advantage, making Adobe XD very important and potentially the leading UX design tool for the days to come.

Ease of Use

Those familiar with digital designing may have used an Adobe application and are somewhat acquainted with the general interface: tool panel on the left, the main area in the center, layers, etc., on the right. The attraction of Adobe XD is that you will feel comfortable as soon as you start using it. The learning curve is slight and occurs primarily around more complex design systems and symbol overrides.

Like other likeminded tools, Adobe XD also handles complex design systems and symbol libraries. Moreover, it features intuitive tools for smoothly connecting screens and creating interactive prototypes that can be used in user testing without any code. The recent release of auto-animate allows prototyping rich interactions even simpler by automatically animating micro-interactions all over the artboards in Adobe XD.

Ecosystem

One of its most vital selling points is having an Adobe XD in the Abode ecosystem because chances are you already have Creative Cloud or use other Adobe products weekly. From vectors to photos, the suite of Adobe products has a dedicated tool for most designer needs that will work pretty smoothly with Adobe XD.

- **What is Adobe XD system requirements?** To use the software, you have to be aware of Adobe XD's minimum system requirements.

  If Mac is your OS, you'll be required to be running Mac OS X or 10.11 and later versions.

- **Can it possible to work Adobe XD on a non-retina display?** Yeah, of course, But it's highly suited that you have to use it on a retina display to avail XD's on-point interface.

  Adobe XD can only run on Windows 10 (Anniversary Update) or later, if your tool of choice is Windows (Windows 7 and XP users, no way, sorry.)

  Additionally, Adobe XD is available in German, Japanese, English, French, and Korean.

Adobe XD Features

With XD, you will be able to start with low-fidelity Wireframes and then change to high-fidelity Mockups. You can also link artboards, set interactions, and make your prototype to the public so you will be able to receive feedback, all without leaving the app.

You can also work with multiple artboards in XD as much like Sketch and Photoshop CC.

When you set off your project, it is possible to select from preset sizes for the most common mobile and web resolutions, or it can be possible to create a custom artboard size.

Can You Move Artboards in Adobe XD?

Moving an artboard by clicking the name tab above the artboard and dragging it into any position you want on the screen is possible. The artboard and contents included in it will all move collectively, so you don't require to drag each element individually or club them all along.

If you have your artboards in place, you will be able to rearrange them, whatever you would like to assist you in visualizing user flow and organizing its order on your screens.

What Can You Do on Artboards?

You will be able to copy and move elements between artboards, freely moving them by dragging and dropping them between designs. You can also marquee-select multiple artboards to cut, copy, edit, or delete them at once.

Create and Use Grids for Layouts

Adobe XD also give you the capability to add grids to place elements in the artboard you created.

Two types of grid options:

1. **Square grids.**

2. **Layout grids.**

Square grids are pretty helpful when you have guides to align text objects. When you draw a shape, its edges will instinctively snap to the grid, assuring you that it is on point.

But in the case of layout grids, it allows you to define columns in your artboard. A layout grid is convenient for understanding how each element responds to different breakpoints—a fundamental need for responsive designs.

Adobe XD Design and Prototype Mode Features
Two modes that you can work within Adobe XD:

1. **Design.**

2. **Prototype.**

Wireframes, visuals, and low and high-quality Mockups are created by using Design Mode. On the other hand, Prototype Mode is to add interactions that simulate the flow of your project.

What Can You Do in Design Mode?
You can easily create your layouts, Wireframes, and the visual design of your project in Design Mode.

Here, using all of your standard objects such as:

- **Shape Tool:** shortcut to drawing a perfect circle, square, and other geometric shapes can be possible.

- **Select Tool:** have to select a single object or multiple objects to group together.

- **Line Tool:** if we need to draw straight quickly but perfectly horizontal, diagonal, and vertical lines.

- **Vector Pen Tool:** it is used to trace outlines and images or draw freehanded, many complex shapes.

- **Text Tool:** it is for using insert headlines, copy and paragraph text in your design.

- **Crop Tool:** this kind of tool is used to adjust the ratio of bitmap images like photos or downloaded graphics.

- **Zoom Tool:** get a nearer view to edit the exact details in your design.

You have to click and drag anywhere on the page if you want to draw a shape, and as you add more to the screen, XD's smart guides will provide you with exact snapping to line up corners and space objects evenly.

Adobe XD has also adapted layers as much as Photoshop and Illustrator but have been re-imagined for UX designers.

Layers Panel

Each object in your project includes its layer—so no need to manually group each object onto different layers. You can group, duplicate, hide, lock, rename, export, and create symbols within layers.

Since you can work with different artboards in your project, only the layers related to the selected artboard will be projected so that your layers panel will stand clean.

Whenever you work with shapes in Adobe Illustrator, then, of course, you'll be able to see that by using Boolean operations, how similar it is to create complex shapes in XD by combining groups of objects.

You will be able to combine simple shapes and make a compound object by adding to a shape area, subtracting from it, intersecting shape areas, and removing overlapping shape areas.

In Adobe XD, you can also hide objects. Masked portions of your assets so you can turn your attention to an exciting element in your design. This also works great when working with images that you need to crop but still have their actual dimensions inside the hid area.

Benefit of XD is how you will be able to add blur effects to an element. It is almost like masking objects; adding a blur effect is not destructive, and it is possible to recover the original component or image in its exact form.

Creating Assets and Symbols

Assets in Adobe XD works in a very similar way as like creating symbols in Sketch.

We are familiar with that some elements will be used across multiple artboards while designing projects.

You will be able to save an element as an asset or group layers to create a symbol. You can access your assets and symbols without any lag to reuse them across your artboards when saved.

Here are some different assets you can create:

- **Colors:** it is to create a global color scheme to use across your design.

- **Character Styles:** reuse sizes, colors, font styles, and weights in your copy.

- **Symbols:** it is used to create and group objects that are all synchronized together when you are going to make a change to one.

Assets provide you enhanced control over the elements in your design that you end up using continuously across different pages or screens. Any changes you will make will sync to every other instance of that created symbol within your design.

Take an example, and you have to use a header for all your different pages or screens while designing websites or apps

What will you do if you've already designed 20 different screens and now you want to change the background color of your header?

You will be able to create the header as a symbol, make the change in one place, and all the rest will dynamically change to match.

Repeat Grid

If you are an ardent fan of Craft's Duplicate feature, then you can get excited about Adobe XD's Repeat Grid.

It is a timesaver feature where you can duplicate elements with a simple click and drag. The Repeat Grid even provides you the freedom to accommodate your margins between each copy.

This will help you if you're going to design heavily repeated items like lists, cards, and photo galleries.

- **How to export your assets?** Another benefit you would get from Adobe XD is its ability to export production-ready assets.

  Created assets in your design can be exported in PNG, SVG, JPG, and even PDF formats.

- **Adobe XD review of how to export designs:** Take an example that now you're going to design a native app; then you will be obliged to provide the development team with retina-ready assets designed at 1x, 2x, and 3x sizes.

- **Adobe XD review of the export retina:** When you are working with vector elements, then you will be able to design in a 1:1 ratio; after that, XD will export them in different kinds of sizes without making any compromise in their quality.

- **What can you do in Prototype mode?** If you need to make your artboards interactive without needing third-party apps, Switching to Prototype Mode is the best suitable option, that is why Adobe XD separates from other design software like Sketch.

  Sketch also can link artboards and create interactive animations in their latest feature set.

Adobe XD Review of Prototype Mode

By using wires and transitions, you can able to determine user flow.

XD lets you visually connect your screens using wires.

Adobe XD Review of Artboard Wires

The wires are a connection point that provides you with how pages or screens link to one another.

If a user clicks on a linked object by using this. You will be able to create transitions between linked objects.

You will be able to target an artboard to transition to, select the transition effect and making of the transition with easing, and the end; you can also choose how long it is required for the transition effect to last with the duration setting for the clickable object.

Adobe XD Review of Prototype Transitions

This kind of interactivity with prototyping allows you to visualize the UX in your design in one application, which will save your time on website and app development.

Using the Preview Feature

You will be able to accurately preview your artboards to see your complete design along with your screen transitions when you are using Prototype Mode.

You can preview them on a device connected to your computer or by using the in-app Preview feature.

Adobe XD Review of Prototype Preview

For the Preview feature to work, you have to work on a Mac and ensure that your iPhone or Android is connected via USB.

You will be able to preview your screens in real-time if you download the Adobe XD iPhone or Android app, even while you're making any kind of changes in your designs.

Another exciting feature is XD's built-in screen recording.

The screen recording feature allows you to record a screencast video of the interactions between your prototypes, but unfortunately, it works on Mac only.

Adobe XD Screen Recording Workaround Hack for Windows
There are some kinds of workarounds to do screen recordings

in XD on Windows computers, but no headway in this regard so far.

Windows's built-in recorder is helpful here. If you want to use it, press the Windows + G keys to bring up the native recorder, then press the Win + Alt + R keys to set off the recording design prototype Preview window.

Adobe XD Windows Screen Recording Hack for Windows 10

- **Adobe XD Collaboration Tools:** The normal UI design process usually goes something like this:

  - **Design > Prototype > Share > Get Feedback > Revise.**

Web and app designers were forced to use multiple tools to complete this process before.

For example, tools like Photoshop, Sketch, and Illustrator used by web designers in design, and for prototyping, separate tools like Axure, Marvel, and InVision and sharing.

All kind of steps you need in the design process are integrated into one app is what make Adobe XD so attractive. You will also be able to share it with others right away after you have completed your project.

There are three ways to collaborate on projects:

1. You will be able to publish your prototype using a public link by sharing via Slack, email, or any other kind of team collaboration tool you are familiar with.

2. If you want to publish your design specs and share them with developers, it is also possible. (This kind of feature is still in beta, so you could run into bugs or hard work as intended.)

All of your links are placed in the Adobe Cloud, so you can manage your published links online whenever you want from any computer.

- If you are not comfortable with your published prototypes and design specs, then there is an option to delete them.

Adobe is not static, and it's constantly adding new features set. You have to be updated to get all of Adobe XD's latest features. That is available on their websites.

Using UI Kits and Third-Party Extensions
Adobe XD does currently back a few third-party extensions.

These extensions are available only in Mac OS, sad news for Windows owners. Hope this can be updated.

Although their third-party extensions—Sympi, ProtoPie, Zeplin, Avocode, and Kite Compositor—are few, a significant benefit in extending XD's functionality.

We can take a look at some of Adobe XD's 3rd Party tools:

- **Sympli:** Sympli gives teams with an integrated experience in Adobe XD All members from developers, designers, managers, and QA professionals have a very light collaboration through linked comments, designs, annotations, and mentions.

- **ProtoPie:** ProtoPie helps design ideas into highly interactive prototypes for designers. With designers can mock up real-world interactions with the help of ProtoPie's on-screen micro-interactions within minutes.

- **Zeplin:** Zeplin automatically grabs all the necessary annotations like colors, margins, sizes as it's a kind of collaboration tool and even CSS suggestions to let work between developers and designers.

- **Avocode:** Avocode allows designers to inspect designs, export images up to @4x, and hand-off layer styles as CSS, Swift, and Android code.

- **Kite Compositor:** The most potent Kite app is a prototyping tool. You can visually drag-and-drop layers to build complex interfaces, add animations within the integrated timeline. You can also use the built-in JavaScript scripting to magnify the details.

Currently, a whole number of UI kits are available in the market for Adobe XD to help designers who want to increase their design process.

How to Use Adobe XD UI Kits
Few standard UI kits of XD are available for designers to use.

- **What are UI kits?** Although UI elements, like lists, avatars, and checkboxes, have simplistic designs, recreating these elements repeatedly is a time-consuming task.

  If you need to use your designs to mock up app-like interfaces quickly, you can use these UI kits, a pre-designed set of UI elements. Using a UI kit provides you access to an assortment of web design and native app UI components like icons, keyboard layouts, navigation bars, buttons, inputs, and more.

Ready-made UI resources will provide you with a head start on your designs; it also helps you develop visually outstanding and accurate designs for just about any device interface.

Ways to Download and Import UI Kits into Adobe XD

You can download from the Menu and open UI kits for Apple iOS, Microsoft Windows, and Google Material Design.

Other cool UI kits curated for Smartwatch, Facebook, etc., are currently out there for download.

If you want to import UI kits into Adobe XD, then you need to copy UI components you preferred into artboards, then you can customize them in any way you wish.

XD Guru provides several free UI Kits for exclusive users of Adobe XD.

Adobe XD iOS UI Kit

You will be able to download an iOS UI kit into XD if you are planning to design an iOS native app.

The iOS UI kit provides you comprehensive UI resources with the full range of commands, views, and glyphs icons used on the iPhone. These preconfigured asset groups are beneficial in maintaining a standardized iOS feel in your UI designs.

Adobe XD Material Design UI Kits

If you're designing for Android devices, Components sticker sheets meant for Material Design are available for download.

These sticker sheets include the latest versions of Material Design's components such as light and dark symbols, layouts, app bars, toolbars, cards, floating action buttons, menus, and more.

Adobe XD-Like Software Alternatives

XD is a great app, but it does have some limitations that may be a deal-breaker for you. Like the significant deal-breaker is that it is a subscription-only service and required to sign up with Adobe's Creative Cloud for its use.

Other Adobe XD-like software alternatives like InVision (Currently only supports Mac and iOS), Figma (Supports Mac, Windows, and Linux), and Marvel (Currently only supports Mac and iOS), also give you the ability to design Mockups and prototypes, and these apps offer both free and premium (paid) versions.

Adobe XD's Issues and Bugs

Even though Adobe XD is updated regularly (like every month since its beta version), it is sure to run into some issues.

Most common bugs to watch out for:

When you are using XD, you may face frequent freezes and crashes, resulting in unsaved projects.

The mysterious Error 44, where you may end up in trouble uploading your prototypes in the app. This is the result of a slow network connection, or it may be that you somehow got disconnected while sharing your prototype.

Adobe XD Review of Common Bugs and Errors

There is a possibility of a bug when panning across your design with the space bar in your Windows 10.

Here are some other minor issues:

- Some keyboard hotkeys not working.

- Changes to stroke and shadow elements while using the Repeat Grid.

- Sometimes, when importing files from Illustrator, there's a bug with the style properties not rendering correctly.

However, if you do run into any of these issues, the good news is that Adobe XD has its feedback platform where you can report bugs and crashes (and make feature requests).

So far, the Adobe XD community is actively posting feedback and bugs, and the XD developers are busy responding and filing these issues. So, hopefully, they will make it on the roadmap to make future updates even more reliable.

The Verdict: Is Adobe XD useful for you?

So, with that being said, should you use Adobe XD for your next project?

The simple answer is…it all depends on you, the designer.

Adobe XD Pros and Cons

Some pros and cons to help you make that decision:

- **Pros:**

  - Design Mockups, prototypes and collaborate all in one app.

  - Redesigned layers panel that puts each object on its layer.

- Prototype wires feature to link artboards.

- Built-in screen recording feature (only for Mac).

- **Cons:**

  - No built-in diagramming features.

  - Must sign up with Adobe Creative Cloud and pay the subscription cost.

  - No built-in code management to handoff to developers.

  - No support for Linux operating system.

  - No-touch/gesture support for prototypes

  - Currently only supports a few third-party apps and a limited number of extensions.

Conclusion

In conclusion, there are many great design and prototyping tools to choose from, but, if the pros outweigh the cons, it would be better.

B. MOCKPLUS

Mockplus is a rapid prototyping tool that helps you to simplify complexity on UI design. It is a desktop-based software tool that supports software prototyping on multiple major platforms, such as mobile-based, desktop-based, and website-based applications. Pre-built widgets and components are available. In addition, it lets you customize widgets, features, and templates; export HTML and PNG files; and print prototype pages. Prototypes can be previewed by scanning QR codes.

Mockplus is a common prototyping tool.

With the help of drag-and-drop WYSIWYG edit, Mockplus will create interactive linking between pages and components. It also supports rapid interactive prototyping in minutes with a simple interface to design prototypes/ Mockups; no coding experience is required. It is also an all-in-one web-based product design platform that provides:

- High-fidelity interactive prototyping.

- Simple developer handoff.

- Real-time collaboration.

- Scalable yet reusable design systems.

Your entire product design workflow can be connected into one place. The more exciting part of this is its capability to bring all participants on the same page, like developers, designers, product managers, clients, stakeholders, and other design participants, to design faster and collaborate better.

We can start designing quickly using Mockplus's built-in online prototyping tool, as there are several ready-to-use icons, UI components, and templates. Animations, interactions, transitions, responsive layouts, and real-time co-editing like innovative vector tools will help you create mobile app prototypes or websites that work like the real thing.

If you need to import existing designs from any design tools (like Adobe XD, Photoshop, Figma, Axure, and Sketch) to proceed on your design workflow, collaborate with your team, review and leave comments on the screen and transfer all design specs, code snippets, assets, and other deliverables to developers only by a simple link.

Mockplus let product managers and designers work comfortably online, as its ability to reduce the gap between designers and developers ultimately. A much better explanation is possible though quickly writing or importing a PRD online and referring to the documents and other related design pages collectively. It also helps you with the help of drag and drop to overview all pages of a project in one place and create a user flowchart based on the project pages.

Your entire team will gather and maintain a unified design system is another feature of Mockplus. Import components, fonts, icons, colors, and other assets from design tools like Sketch. It can be reused instantly from anywhere by other team members at any time.

Even though it is a new player in the prototyping field, Mockplus has emerged as a real stand-out thus far with a competent team from the orient supported. Instead of overemphasizing functionalities, this agile design tool does give UX the highest priority, making sure anyone of every level can prototype faster, smarter, and more accessible. Its user-centric interaction and highly intuitive interface have gained an increasing number of global customers. If you want to check your app Mockup for free, then you must use the Mockplus app. This tool offers its users 300 plus tools to design swiftly and efficiently.

- Supports interactive prototype.

- Designers, Developers, and Managers can collaborate easily.

- Dynamic and reusable design systems.

- Share, Manage, and Maintain with ease.

Mockplus is a one-stop online design platform that helps you to do everything from prototyping to developer hand-off. Turn your ideas into testable and deliverable designs in one place.

A whole number of valuable components are already built-in Mockplus. Things like image carousels popups and scroll boxes will allow your prototype to be interactive from the onset.

Assembling it using their simple drag-and-drop inter-face is one of its exciting parts as there is no code here.

In terms of its built-in assets, Version 2.19 (Pro) significantly evolved. It will introduce nearly 3,000 icons from its earlier 400. All newly introduced icons will be in vector format to be sharp at any size and font. Whatever you need is placed in one place, so you no longer need to search around for icons to use in your project.

The time-saving Auto Recovery feature is one of the new features. Using this feature, you can create interactive commands based on things like page loading and user clicks by using Mockplus.

You can restore the original interaction once the first interaction occurs with the help of Auto Recovery. It requires just a couple of mouse clicks, so you don't need to invest maximum time by tirelessly doing copy and paste.

Preview and Export with Ease

Whenever you create your prototype, it will be easy to review it on your mobile device. So you need to scan the generated QR code, and the device will download your project automatically. You can even use it while offline. For making the whole process fast and easy, the Pro version uses cloud sync. Use and share your prototype without needing a USB cable or having to email a large file.

You will get options whenever you want to export your project. It is available to export your project tree in many popular formats, including Text, Image (Pro), CSV, HTML, Tree View, Mind Map, Markdown, and XML.

Version 2.19 will let users copy and paste text directly from the exported demo package is another convenient feature.

What Is a Prototype?

A prototype is an early model, sample, or release of a product built to check process or concept or act as a thing to be copied or learned from within.

Term prototype is used in various contexts, including design, electronics, semantics, and software programming. It is used to try and test a new design to increase its precision by system users and analysts. Rather than a theoretical one, prototyping act as a tool of specifications for a real, working system. In some workflow models, creating a prototype, or sometimes this process is called materialization, is a step between the formalization and the evaluation of an idea.

Why Rapid Prototype?

You have to clarify the definition of a prototype before you venture out to design an app, no matter whether it is a desktop or mobile app. It will be helpful to your following work if you have comprehensive knowledge of rapid prototyping.

- First, you can quickly create an early version of a product by rapid prototyping, allowing you to materialize and visualize your ideas.

- Second, it lets designers test ideas intuitively and even gets user feedback quickly, which can help you enhance and perfect the ideas.

- Third, designers will get a feel of the guard through this procedure.

That will help designers be time-saving, economically, and effortlessly before the release of the final product.

Anyway, rapid prototyping is an unavoidable method of design works.

Relationship between Prototype and Mockplus?

We have learned from the above introduction that Mockplus is a professional prototyping tool that is helpful to UI/UX designers. Put another way, Mockplus is the best choice for application prototyping, and undoubtedly, it is Mockplus that is the most effective prototyping tool.

More Impressive Features of Mockplus

- **Simplism style:** The spirit of the Mockplus team is supplying the best services on prototyping elaborate ideas with a simple tool. That's the concept of simplism. The desktop Mockplus displays a simple interface formed by three main parts: component and widget library, working space, project panel. Despite such a concise and clear layout structure, Mockplus is more powerful than it can be imagined. No specialized knowledge on coding and programming is required; users can quickly and effectively create application prototyping. Moreover, it does not take too much time to learn the usage of this simple tool. Rather than wasting unnecessary time on tool learning, generating more wonderful and ingenious ideas is better.

- **Abundant icons and components:** Mockplus Pro offers almost 200 pre-designed elements that let you work even faster and easier. Rich elements offer users extensive choices for their design work, which can be a good reason for labor-saving. Besides, the 400+ icons (with even more coming soon) are enough to help create prototypes.

- **Optional prototyping styles:** Users can choose two styles when opening Mockplus, sketch, and Wireframe. Designers can work in any style you prefer. Some enjoy the sketch or hand-drawn style because that just adds to the authenticity of the prototyping.

Online Designing and Prototyping

With the help of ready-made components, icons, and templates with Mockplus, we can create a lifelike prototype.

You can create custom logos, images, components, and illustrations using vector tools. If you want to customize elements with advanced style editing modes, it is also possible. For making a realistic prototype, create different animations, interactions, and transitions with its drag-and-drop functionality and build a rich page or component states. Collaboration is not challenging as we can co-edit the designs team you are working within real-time.

Design Collaboration

One of the most exciting features of Mockplus is its ability to completely avoid time-consuming by reviewing designs continuously with your team and leaving a comment directly on screens. You will create and manage design tasks to have a complete hand in your design and review process. The PRDs that you created online are also connected with related design pages. Mockplus will help you to manage teams and projects with more accessible roles. If you want to keep track of your team and project activities, the Auto-notifications option will help you to monitor

Design Handoff

You will be able to design right from Photoshop, Sketch, Adobe XD, Figma, and Axure. You can then transfer designs to developers with auto specs, code snippets, assets, and many more. To start coding quickly, you can download all assets and code snippets in one click.

Design System

Mockplus allows you to gather and manage the design system with your team online. Integrate with design tools like Sketch to import colors, components, fonts, and more. You can share and reuse design assets across your team and link projects and design systems for fast coding.

UX designers or researchers always keep looking for new technologies, even though some people tend to go vanilla and create a prototype by hand using paper and pen. Designers are not in a mood to use the sophisticated tool if they can make it a more accessible alternative. These are some highlighted features of Mockplus that will help your design process to the new horizon with minimum effort.

Fully Visualized Interaction

Interaction design relies on creating an engaging interface with well-planned behaviors. It is drag and drop based at Mockplus, which helps you build interactive prototypes in a completely visualized way, with no repetitive selection or calculation needed.

The Link Point on each component sets up interactive components, and a link between pages, in-page, or cross-page is not a problem.

If we need to make a movable picture when the "Adjust" button is clicked, just click on the button component and drag the Link Point to the required picture. Once you have completed it, a dialog window will pop up on the screen to prompt you to define a command for your component.

Ready-Made Components

Pre-designed and readily available components will minimize the overall design time and considerably enhance quality. There are more than 200 ready-made components specifically curated to fit both web and mobile apps in Mockplus, making the interactive design less time-consuming. The newly added components contain an image carousel, stack panel, scroll box, popup panel, sliding drawer, and more.

For example, you can attain scrolling for a web prototype by simple drag and drop in the scroll box. another enhanced way to set scrolling for a mobile prototype with header and footer area fixed.

New Features Wrapped in V2.19

Mockplus also keeps improving and evolving rather rapidly like any other tool on the market, with a remarkable set of new features included in each update. In the case of version 2.19, there are four spotlights that you must not turn your head away:

1. **3,000 Vector-Based Icons:** A total of 3,000 icons are out there for free use, with 400 flat icons and 2,500+ vector icons included. It is all are outstanding quality and support proportionally scale.

2. **Auto-Recovery Option:** This type of interactive command permits you to restore the original interaction after the first interaction occurs, even though only one touch of the button can return to the initial interaction.

3. **Export to Project Tree:** There will be a high-level view of page flows and choose to export to various file

forms, ranging from Mind Map, Tree View to CSV (opened in Excel), Text, and XML.

4. **Copy Text from the Demo Package:** It can copy all the required text from the demo package by dragging the marquee on the prototype page. For UI designers and developers, it is a kind of time-saver.

Selectable "Wireframe" & "Sketch" Style

You will be able to decide on a style for the Mockup when you are giving your design. The Wireframe style adopts geometrically minimized shapes, while the Sketch style takes on a hand-drawn outlook. Mockplus lets you switch between the two styles with ease.

Multiple Choices to Preview on Any Device

Not only does Mockplus allow designers to make interactive prototypes of their mobile, desktop, or web apps all of a sudden, but it also provides a flexible view of prototypes on any device, in a web browser, or on a mobile device using the Mockplus app for Android and iOS.

Two flexible ways can be chosen if you want to make a mobile demo for completed sketches:

1. **Scanning the Generated QR Code**

2. **Publishing to the Cloud**

Such a device preview will provide you instant feedback on how a layout works on vivid screens.

Pricing Policy and Exclusive Offer

The pricing of Mockplus is like "Pay as you go," as there is a monthly or annual plan to enjoy rapid prototyping on the web, mobile, and desktop platforms. The monthly subscription is available at \$20/mo, but there will be an exclusive 50% discount for the yearly plan, which costs \$119 only. The "Group Purchase" option is also available for anyone who wants three or more copies of this software for team use, offering up to 40% discount with no tied contract.

So if you are a teacher, student, or educator invested in UI/UX design or other software design training-related positions, you will get a FREE trial of the Mockplus Pro version. So what you need is to submit your request, and they will contact you.

Technical and Documentation Support

It's crucial to have reliable documentation and technical support to help your work.

Mockplus treats every user and treats their own family with efficiency and professionalism, so never leave any customer stranded and helpless. It has been acclaimed for informative and responsive support since its first inception.

The Mockplus latest new update is now online. To better enhance your experience, new features and plugins have been added to Exporting your PRD to PDF, copying CSS code bylines together.

Export an Online Written PRD to PDF

Mockplus now have a new "Export to PDF" feature, which lets you export your PRD file to PDF with just one click. Sharing your curated drafts with your partners will be easier with a universally recognizable PDF format. So the discussion in these regards will be much productive.

If your partners are also part of your Mockplus project, you can also share the PRD directly with a secure link instead.

Improved Editing

In the recent update, also improved the online PRD editor. Enter the PRD editing mode to allow you to have the full-screen interface fully revised and optimized for your requirement. Add content, insert images, links, designs, and other media freely for further explanation, and click on "Save" to save them all.

Decide Who Joins the Team

Through these updates, it has implemented the system where the project Admin will be able to accept or deny users' requests to join the team to ensure the safety of your projects. The Admin will get a notification on the home page every time a new user joins a team.

Customize Project Tree

It was not easy to see long page names on the Project Tree panel in the previous versions in some instances. This problem has been addressed in this update, so now you can freely drag panel borders to fit the size.

Copy CSS Code Line by Line

Mockplus can also automatically analyze layers and generate the related style CSS code, which you will be able to copy in just a single click. New updates introduced new features, which let you copy CSS code byline at a time. That does mean when you only require the style CSS codes of one color or height of your designs, you are allowed to copy it in a straightforward click. Copying all CSS codes is not required.

Rename Assets

A new feature has been allowed to enhance the workflow that lets you rename assets in one click. This will be useful when you have several assets to download and manage on your screen. You have to click on the pencil icon next to the title to rename it and put everything in order.

Export WebP Images

Updated Mockplus supports exporting WebP images so that you can export to 3 formats: SVG, WebP, and PNG. You are free to choose one, two, or three formats as per your needs.

In case you're experiencing problems with this function, you can use the Chrome browser.

Change Guide Colors

By default, when you use Development mode, Mockplus uses red color guides to indicate the distance between two objects on the screen. This may cause trouble; you can choose between 3 options: Blue & Red, Purple, and Orange & Blue to sort out these issues and increase readability.

Attach Description to Your Upload

Mockplus now has an "Add update note" feature, which you can use to describe your updates in detail.

Once you attach a description, it will be uploaded together with the design and visible to all the teammates in the Activity mode.

Simple and Clean

The interface of Mockplus is very comfortable to use: effective, fast, and easy on the eyes, with almost grays highlighted by oranges. There is usually enough contrast to show the app's various components and icons apart. However, some potential users with weaker vision may have difficulty. "Components" and "Icons," by the way, are the building blocks this app will have you use, with more than 200 components and 3,000 icons, respectively. Components represent the different non-visual things an app will do, from buttons to scroll bars. The selection of available components is solid, but it bears noting that if your app does something specific, there may not be a component to represent that.

Cons

- **Interaction Components:** Even though Mockplus is very rapid and simple at creating prototypes, but comparatively speaking, it is a little bit weak than other prototypes/Wireframe tool providers at interaction support. To achieve dynamic actions on the current Mockplus 2.0 version needs several steps to do.

However, fortunately, the Mockplus team is well-known for agile development. In the 2.1 version, Mockplus endows outstanding interaction features which are very easy and simple to use. Create interactive prototypes by defining interactions in the Params Panel to set triggers, add Target and Commands. Various interaction modes you can choose freely to realize the effect of what you intended. If you want to execute simultaneous actions, that is no problem, and you only need to know it with a single interaction. The practical interaction feature is very brilliant. Moreover, video tutorials and text tutorials about how to use the interaction feature both are available.

- **Devices Supported:**
  - Windows.
  - Android.
  - iPhone/iPad.
  - Mac.
  - Web-based.
  - Windows mobile.
- **Deployment:**
  - Cloud hosted.
  - On-premise.
- **Language Support:**
  - English.
  - Chinese.
- **Pricing Model:**
  - Monthly payment.
  - One-time payment.
  - Annual subscription.
- **Customer Types:**
  - Small business.
  - Large enterprises.
  - Medium business.
  - Freelancers.

C. MOQUPS

Moqups is a cloud-based visual collaboration software to help organizations create and validate functional prototypes for designing applications and websites. Teams can utilize whiteboard functionality to collaborate on diagrams, Wireframes, and Mockups. The diagramming tools let designers develop sitemaps, storyboards, or flowcharts and cross-navigate among the components. It is another creative collaboration tool that relies on wireframing but can also be used for prototyping. It is mainly web-based and is used to make Wireframes for mobile and web applications.

The main difference of Moqups is its fidelity to the Wireframes. Moqups render you full-color stencils and kits for mobile app and web design, including Android, iOS, and Bootstrap.

Moqups distinguishes itself from others in different ways. The software allows for page management and finite object editing, providing designers the freedom to define "master" objects, which will help time-saving when making required changes to the Wireframes during the iteration process.

Let's take an example if you create a master button object with a specific shape, size, and color. This button can be used multiple times throughout the Wireframe. In the iteration process, if you need to change the button's color, instead of changing every single button object, they can change it once, and all the child button objects are subsequently affected.

Moqups offers stencil kits, which let users create personalized designs using multiple elements like icons, fonts, shapes, and widgets from a built-in library. Features include roles and permissions management, activity audit logs, private projects, single sign-on (SSO), multiple teams, and more. Managers can include annotations or comments, modify designs, and communicate via chat, facilitating real-time engagement across projects.

Editing capabilities in Moqups lets users resize, align or rotate objects, bulk edit, rename or lock elements, and adjust specifications using grids, custom guides, rulers, and other alignment tools. It allows integration with different third-party applications, including Google Drive, Slack, and Dropbox.

It is also a visual collaboration program with many tools like design features, whiteboards, and diagrams.

If any companies want to plan, communicate, collaborate, and strengthen people and work management, it's one of the most suitable options.

Emil Tamas launched this platform in 2012 and has become one of the stunning tools.

If you want to create a different visual product to support all sorts of projects, Moqups will help you tremendously.

It provides prototypes, Mockups, dashboards, Mind Maps, Wireframes, and many other ways to echo an organization's message.

It is best suited for executives, corporations, UX professionals, technology-based companies, cross-functional teams, marketing and management agencies, and multiple organizations that work on complicated projects. It also helps companies streamline their processes and track progress. For making better team collaboration and enhanced team communication, Moqups added various fascinating features.

A robust kind of design should have powerful prototyping, Mockups, and wireframing. It is inevitable that you pictorial your theories, concepts, mission, and vision to make a meaningful impact.

This platform replicates designs and brings them to life with the assistance of different workflows, work charts, and user journeys beforehand.

The information you provide will undoubtedly have a more significant impact on Moqups, with maximum user engagement and productive team collaboration and communication with just one click.

This web design-based tool helps you build all sorts of Mockups, prototypes, and Wireframes for your business. You can make your design more visually appealing and detailed and also navigate between projects and team members.

Another credible choice with flexible drag-and-drop UI, Moqups, is famous as a wireframing tool for interaction design flows. Developers can place icons and images from its built-in library and personal folders into projects. A unique Diagram tool in Moqups lets users make logical markups on the Wireframe to identify where links and interactions will live or even how the UX logic will flow within the app design.

Moqups provide multiple-platform integration like Android, iOS, Web, macOS, and Windows. Stencil kits, a range of stylish fonts, organized pages, and more make Moqups a developer's preferred tool. Moqups's cloud integration lets developers work remotely through Slack, Google Drive, and Dropbox.

Key Features of Moqups

- An ecosystem of different tools.

- Moqups give you diagrams, Wireframes, prototypes, images, fonts, stencils, icons, and others. It is not required to change one platform to use different features like page management, constructing images, or object editing.

- This kind of streamlined experience helps your work quicker, easier, and more straightforward.

- Flexible, scalable, powerful features.

The features provided by Moqups features are flexible, scalable, and robust. They enhance as your business develops. With this platform, you will be able to handle projects of any size and length; its drag-and-drop builder is advanced, and navigation is not complicated.

- Editing and creating graphics/images from scratch are precise, fast, intuitive, and loaded with dynamic tools.

- Built-In Library with Graphics and Fonts.

- Thousands of icon sets are attached to the built-in library.

- Ready-to-use stencils designed for widespread use cases and custom stencil kits for Android and iOS mobile app design are available.

- Resize, align, style, or rotate objects. You will also be able to group, bulk-edit, lock and rename elements. With the help of custom guides, rulers, and grids, precise adjustments can be made.

You can choose hundreds of fonts from the integrated Google Font. Advanced controls allow you to tweak the text to match your designs.

Organize Your Projects

Drag and drop your pages to organize or reorder them in folders.

Search and navigate through your folders will be accessible through the option of Pages Panel.

You will be able to auto-apply changes to all associated pages with the help of Master Pages.

Integrations and Collaboration

We already discussed that Moqups has integrations with tools like Google Drive, Dropbox, and Slack.

Even if you are working remotely, your team can collaborate because of the cloud.

You will get feedback right on the design itself and make edits without sending various versions to one another.

Accelerates Your Creativity

You will be able to maintain your team's focus in Moqups by helping creativity with automation. It provides a comprehensive range of styles, icons, fonts, stencils, and more selected from within. It keeps you on alert. This platform lets you keep everybody aware—from business analysts to designers, stakeholders to employees, and managers to developers.

Work from Anywhere

You can work from anywhere as it is cloud-based and supported on all devices—from laptops, desktops to mobile phones. Geographical constraints are not a concern here as everyone is in line with Moqups' quick upload and download feature.

Built-in Library for Icons and Stencils

This platform has a library of icons that is accessible to everyone. You will be able to drag and drop any image speedily you wish to replace, preserve the size, and position it the way you want to, without any constraints.

It also provides a comprehensive collection of innovative shapes, widgets, and stencils that make your design more scintillating. You can also choose from different stencils and add them to both the mobile and web design.

Team Collaboration and Communication

One of the tremendous significance of Moqups is to simplify your team's communication and collaboration as a whole. Your team will get your message loud and clear when creating diagrams, workflows, Wireframes, and prototypes.

This platform allows you to collaborate in real-time with absolute transparency manner. Integrates with Slack, Dropbox, and Google Drive are helpful here.

Moqups Products

- **Wireframes:** You will be able to make your team understand the organizational hierarchy, the workload of each employee, the user flow of the project, and the density of the page. It also uses placeholder text and simple shapes that will help you to create advanced flow.

  You just focus on the structure; Moqups will take care of everything.

- **Mockups:** This feature lets your team get feedback on the submitted design. You can also build on the Wireframe to visualize the content and function. It acts as a demo process to show clients how their design will be on the main page.

  Mockups allow you to put the designs into context with a result.

- **Diagrams and Flowcharts:** For enhancing employee understanding, it helps you to create diagrams and flowcharts. You can create multiple diagrams, including use-case diagrams, concept diagrams, sitemaps, Mind Maps, decision trees, and flowcharts for vivid workflows.

  This platform gives you a flowchart stencil that you enter the content and extend it. You can also fully customize it.

- **Charts and Graphs:** To simplify communication between employees, graphs and charts play a significant role. It allows you to present visually hitting information.

You can also create area charts, bar charts, doughnut charts, column charts, line charts, pie charts, and much more with the help of Moqups.

- **Online Whiteboard:** Moqups helps your team to collaborate and brainstorm with its online whiteboard feature. Sharing ideas between teammates is allowed in real-time. This visual collaboration tool allows interaction with no constraints and makes your work from your device itself.

  The online whiteboard has advanced sticky notes, freehand drawing, annotations, shapes, and everything else provided with the offline whiteboard experience.

- **UML Diagram Tool:** This feature provides you create powerful visualizations that look professional with a complete UML stencil set. It offers hundreds of templates with real-time collaboration and provides a unified modeling language to match all industry standards. Easily shareable diagrams and can be made within minutes.

  You can select from sequence diagrams, class diagrams, component diagrams, activity diagrams, use-case diagrams, deployment diagrams, profile diagrams, composite structure diagrams, and package diagrams. Hence, it is an all-in-one tool to make your content brilliant.

- **Mockup Templates:** Moqups has many templates you can select from to create the best flowcharts, diagrams, and prototypes. It allows you maintain team momentum by getting spontaneous feedback and robust charts that detail business information to employees.

It also allows your team shares the same vision with robust collaboration, with the help of a unified set of intuitive tools.

Here are some templates on Moqups:

- Price page Wireframe.

- Mobile app landing page Wireframe.

- Mind Maps.

- Sitemaps.

- High- and low-fidelity Wireframe.

- Mobile app Wireframe.

- Blog page Wireframe.

- Wireframes and Mockups for eCommerce websites.

- Admin dashboard Wireframe.

- Landing page Wireframe.

- UML diagrams.

- Process maps.

- ERD diagrams for network, organization, and timelines.

- Bar graphs and chart.

- Line graphs and charts.

- Area graphs and chart.

- Pie and doughnut charts.

- Funnel charts.
- Column graphs and charts.
- Gantt chart.
- Customer journey maps.
- Business model canvas.
- SWOT analysis format.
- Release roadmap.
- Empathy map.
- User person.
- User story mapping.
- Kanban board.
- Affinity diagram.
- Cause and effect diagrams.
- Business strategy templates.
- Storyboard.
- Weekly calendar.
- Eisenhower matrix.
- 4Qs framework.
- 4Ls retrospective.
- Competitor analysis.
- Five whys analysis.

- Daily standup meeting.

- Meeting agenda.

- Growth engine board and much more.

- Free online graph and flowchart maker.

Moqups allow you to turn your raw data and information into engaging and fascinating visual pieces. The online graph maker will enable you to customize with over a thousand images and hundreds of chart templates and icons that fit your audience, mission, brand, and vision.

The features we discussed above are available for free of cost.

But you need to upgrade if you want to share, export, and save a flowchart or graph.

Like big brands in the industry, Amazon, Microsoft, Intel, SONY, and Oracle trusted this chart and graph maker.

Following are the unique features of Moqups:

- It is entirely customizable.

- The option of a drag-and-drop editor allows you to replace anything with a single click.

- It provides you to create charts and graphs within minutes.

- It provides you to create online, collaborate in real-time, and you can work from wherever you want by saving the work on the cloud.

- It allows you to share with your team immediately.

- It shares links online, and they can add them to the dashboards, post them on social media, and export them on the device.

What you need to do is create your own graph/chart:

- The template is according to your preferences.

- Add your data set.

- Style and customize the graphs/charts.

- Share it with the collaborators or export it online.

Moqups Advantages and Disadvantages
Moqups Advantages

- It is an easy-to-use platform, and even a beginner can use it with no hurdles.

- One of the time-consuming tools since it provide templates to create flows and charts quickly.

- It allows you to enhance your creativity with fascinating designs that you can customize.

- It provides unlimited animations, integrations, powerful expressions, and designs not accessible to other competitors.

- Moqups lets you create dynamic Mockups and Wireframes that lead to effective collaboration between multiple employees. It also creates a clear communication channel between top to bottom management levels.

Moqups Disadvantages

- By not sending renewal notifications of the tool, it creates a kind of obstruction. They deduct the cost post the trial period, and refunds are hard to claim.

- The time-consuming factor is its incapability to select all instead of one-by-one elements and edit it with the drag-and-drop editor. Rearranging flowcharts can be the steadiest process.

- For downloading the Mockup, you need to upgrade to the paid plan. These kinds of things obstruct the purpose of having a free plan.

Resources and Blogs

The platform itself has materials and resources that are more useful than you can think. Moqups also includes informative articles on the difference between low and high-fidelity Wireframes, introducing the multiple teams feature, stick and stack containers, the usage, project folders, live chats in Moqups, etc.

Moqups share with you all about the platform. No requirement for a subscription or creating an account for it.

Extensions, Add-Ons, and Integrations

Moqups has a chrome extension to grab screenshots, and use a color selection tool and create projects. You can also save the screenshots directly to your device and make a mood board.

This program was introduced with a Firefox add-on. It provides the same features like the chrome version, enabling eyedroppers, taking screenshots, and seamlessly creating projects.

Last but not least, Moqups has a fantastic set of integrations that allow you to connect to different platforms and make your work quicker, easier, and simpler.

These integrations included Confluence server, Jira Cloud, Confluence Cloud, Jira server, Dropbox, Slack, Google Drive, and many others. All these have their benefits and up your design game with sharper response time and overall excellence.

Following are the steps that will show you the apps and integrations tab on the Moqups platform:

You have to click on the account menu in the top right corner of the app's toolbar, then select account settings and open the accounts setting window in the platform's dashboard. You need to choose the apps and notifications tab.

Then you will get all the available integrations in just one click.

Support

Moqups has a unique support group that is always available for you. You just need to enter your issue into their specific form for any complaints, and they will respond to you promptly. You can add pictures of your problem as well. All in all, their support executives are customer-friendly and will assist you in using the platform.

Moqups Pricing Plans

The Moqups platform was introduced with a free plan and two paid options. The free plan provides you with essential features and does not ask you to enter your payment card or obligations. This opportunity provides you with enough time to venture into the parts and make up your mind if you want to use them further. The paid plans come with outstanding features that help you enhance your collaboration and communication.

The free plan only has one project, which is constrained to 200 objects and 5MB of storage.

All plans include:

- Unlimited projects and objects.

- Prototype interactions.

- Flow diagramming.

- Uploading own designs.

- Quick icon replacement.

- Drag-and-drop editor.

- Easy link sharing.

- Google Drive exporting.

- Real-time comments and editing.

- Annotate designs and note-taking.

- Over one thousand icons from popular libraries.

- Unlimited feedback and comments.

- Quick Wireframe creation.

- Slack notifications.

- Dropbox exporting.

- Creating Trello cards.

- PRO plan.

The pro plan contains five editors and costs $16 per month, billed annually. The plan includes:

- Real-time collaboration.
- Jira and confluence integrations.
- UNLIMITED plan.
- Unlimited objects and projects.
- Private projects.

Roles and Permissions

This is the top-level plan that provides everything. It will be $69 per month (discounted) for unlimited editors, annual subscription.

The plan includes everything in the pro plan:

- Multiple teams.
- Email domain allows list.
- Unlimited members.
- SSO.

Getting Started with Moqups

Getting started up with Moqups is super simple, and it would be better to start with the free account.

- **Creating a Design:** It is fascinating the drag-and-drop editor. In some editors, if you click an element, it immediately pops up on the project, and then it can be troublesome to get rid of. Moqups makes you feel like you have a little bit of control over what you add and lets you explore the options without getting perplexed. You will click something and add it without understanding accidentally; as you drag an element to your project, you will be able to watch what it'll look like and then put it right back if you make up your mind that you don't need it.

- **Working with a Design:** When you hover over the different elements in your design, a blue outline shows you the other page elements. If you want to work with a component, then click to select it. A menu will provide on the right with custom options.

- **Project Colors:** You may like the "Project Colors" part of the color picker. This will give more straightforward to match the color of the heart in the upperleft corner with the color of the text.

- **Saving Elements as Templates:** One of the valuable features of Moqups is that you will be able to save elements as templates, then easily add them to other pages as-is. The original design will be retained – size, color, etc. This allows creating continuity in your design.

- **Collaboration Features:** Commenting will be accustomed to and behave in a way you're familiar with if you are a Google Drive user. Adding a comment will be super cool, and you can also move the comment around before or after writing it so that its placement makes sense.

If you have several collaborators and comments, though, that small comment pane can get out of hand fast. You need to create a rule for your team that comments are marked as resolved when they're no longer required.

Who Is Moqups Best for?

Moqups is much helpful for non-developers to conceptualize during the first stages of project planning. For example, a project manager or business owner can share their idea with the development and design team, using more sophisticated methods to create the actual product or a high-fidelity rendering.

Moqups is especially helpful for Mockups and wireframing, but it's not as powerful when we consider prototyping. Moqups doesn't have many features like other prototyping tools, and styling elements can't be customized in as many ways as competitive tools, either. It's barely even mentioned on their website.

D. MOCKPLUS iDOC

Good collaboration between developers and designers will help a team to reach unimaginable heights in creating products. An integrated online tool/platform for them to collaborate seamlessly is also handy for making things possible. Suppose you set off your journey of career by getting into a new team. In that case, you will encounter the fact that you are not in a vacuum—you become a part of a system called "the process of creating a product" because you have to cooperate with totally different kinds of specialists from different niches—marketing, business, design, etc. All these areas are interconnected and are impossible without each other. Even if you create a perfect code, it is worth nothing if it is not sold appropriately. And a great UX design will allow you to become number one on the market simply because your product is more convenient than others.

We have many tools that help make this communication as convenient as possible for all parties. One of these magic tools is Mockplus iDoc—a robust product design collaboration tool for designers and developers by creating a connected online space for product teams. Designers can export their designs from Adobe, Sketch, and Photoshop, and the tool will certainly prepare all the assets, specifications, and code snippets you require.

Mockplus iDoc, Connect Your Entire

To make a robust online design collaboration solution for designers and developers, Mockplus introduced Mockplus iDoc, a new brand product design collaboration tool, on November 8, 2020.

Mockplus iDoc is a vital product design collaboration tool for developers and designers. It provides a connected online space for product collaborators. It is not just design workflow but also allows teams with the design handoff. It highly facilitates the handoff by taking designs from

Sketch, Photoshop, and Adobe XD and exporting them into a format that will help team members generate style guides, code snippets, specs, and assets.

Designers will be able to hand off designs with accurate specs, code snippets, assets, and interactive prototypes automatically with the help of Mockplus iDoc.

It is the ultimate online design collaboration tool between developers and designers. All kinds of product design workflow, from design to development, can be connected, and your entire team can focus on building outstanding products together.

Mockplus iDoc is a popular all-in-one online design collaboration tool that lets developers, designers, and product managers import, prototype, test, share, and handoff web/app designers with automatic specs, code snippets, assets.

The product team can easily import designs from Sketch/PS/XD, create UI flows and interactive prototypes, check and download design assets/specs/code snippets, upload and preview files from Axure/JustinMind/Mockplus/Office/Excel, handoff designs, and manage team members with ease.

Its advanced team and project management feature is also worth trying.

Price: Basic free (5 projects and five team members); Professional $9/month.

Why Choose Mockplus iDoc?

Mockplus iDoc is a handy online design collaboration and handoff tool for designers, developers, and product managers to upload, prototype, comment, test, share, and handoff designs with automatic specs, assets, code snippets.

Here are key features of Mockplus iDoc:

- Import designs with automatic specs, assets, code snippets from Sketch, XD, and PS.

- Create UI flow and interactive prototypes with drag and drop.

- Comment, review, test, and iterate designs with simple clicks.

- Check, copy, and download design specs, assets, and code snippets with one click.

- Upload prototypes from Justinmind/Axure/Mockplus and documents.

- You can make a Handoff design with accurate specs, code snippets, and assets with just a click.

It will not be a mountainous claim if we say that Mockplus iDoc is ahead of any other similar tools you've ever accustomed. Take a deep to find out what makes it unique.

Various Ways of Accessing Specs

iDoc provides three specs modes. You can maintain any layers; single or multiple layers also can be selected; you can hold down Alt to convert specs to percentage values.

- **Details of Specs:** Some design details would be too short. You will hold down the Z key in iDoc, and the Magnifier will appear to provide you with detailed specs.

- **View Duplicate Elements:** To get a view of duplicate design elements like text, color, margin, and width with just one click. All duplicate items will be pop up on the screen, and this will, of course, let you enhance work efficiency.

- **Tailored Resources, All in One Place:** Mockplus creates accurate specs, code snippets, and assets from your designs-all of them are adapted for the platform you're developing for. It also automatically converts units according to your project type. Nothing will be lost in design files.

- **Build Your Team's Design Style Guide:** Team projects and resources will be collected and organized automatically. Colors, components, and text styles – all of them will be in the easy-to-maintain style guide.

- **Show Relations in Full-View Storyboard:** Your product complete design screen will be included in the entire view storyboard. If you want to zoom in/out to get all in details, it is also provided. You will be able to make a bond between screens by dragging & dropping a Line between them. By adding a Line description, it will give more details. Fast positioning will become possible with the help of a navigation map.

- **Comments with Various Styles:** IDoc gives various comment styles for your comments, including Circle, Rectangle, Straight Line, Pin Arrow, Text. You can get instant feedback as comments are available in real-time, which will help you move projects forward.

- **Hi-Fi Interactive Prototype:** You can transform your static files into working prototypes smoothly. IDoc has nine transition animations, and it supports auto jumping and setting a fixed area. Group and manage design screens can be handled in the Screen Tree, and it will help to group easily. The structure is evident at a glance.

- **Control Your Project Progress Easily:** You will be able to combine icons (20 icons provided) with colors to mark progress, show priority, or give a comment on designs. It is also allowed to sort design screens visually.

- **Keep Everyone on the Same Page:** IDoc gives a flexible space to share all documents with team members throughout the entire design process. You upload product documents (Axure/Justinmind/Mockplus), and your team members can download or preview them online. All documents can be grouped.

  - Designers can hand off designs effortlessly.

  - Export designs with one click from Adobe XD, Sketch, and Adobe Photoshop.

  - Handoff designs with accurate assets, specs, and code snippets automatically.

  - It will provide feedback and up-to-date comments promptly.

  - If there are any changes required, import and update your existing design again.

- To build your team's design repository, collect and organize a style guide, automatically.

- Product managers can review projects seamlessly.

- Connect and show the bond between each page in a full-view storyboard.

- To communicate effortlessly, gather instant feedback, and move projects forward, add comments right on design.

- If you're completed to keep things organized, then categorize tasks by color and resolve them.

- With the help of your actual design files, create hi-fi interactive prototypes with various animation effects given.

- Support uploading of different kinds of product documents and oversee online.

- Designers write code more productively.

- Accessing and browsing specs in multiple ways is simple.

- Create development resources instinctively, package and download a different kinds of assets.

- Choose the platform you're going to develop, and iDoc will, of course, generate adapted resources.

- Duplicate design elements can be seen quickly with just one click.

- Get pixel-perfect code snippets that are convenient with a click, so apprehension about any loss in translation is minimized.

- Teamwork can be performed more effortlessly.

- Navigate complete design process in one place, act as the perfect collaboration tool from design to development.

- Keep product managers, designers, and engineers working efficiently and effortlessly.

- Group and manage teams and projects, set variety of roles to members different permissions.

A new path for Mockplus has been opened up with the launch of Mockplus iDoc. Product design collaboration is inevitable for product teams. It also provides effective ways to improve work efficiency and focus on the design itself. In the future, Mockplus will continue to polish product details and provide faster and more accessible product design solutions for creators of UX.

New Features of Mockplus iDoc

- **Gesture interaction:** You will have more choices rather than the simple click and jump triggering mode. Mockplus iDoc provides a different kinds of gesture interactions:

  Doubleclick, OnLoad, Press, and Swipe up/down/left/right. These productive gesture interactions make prototype demos more practical

- **Double-click a layer to create an interaction:** You might have faced trouble with making the link area as big as the button when adding an interaction when creating an earlier interaction. This issue has been sorted out. Now you will be able to create a link area by double-clicking a layer directly.

Not only that, whenever a shape of a layer is changed in PS and Sketch after reuploading, the shape of its link area will also be matched to the latest state, and the interaction will also remain.

- **Drag & drop a folder or zip to upload:** Just drag-and-drop folders, images, and zip files directly to the storyboard, instead of an earlier version of unzipping and uploading photos one by one. They will be automatically parsed according to their directory structures.

- **@ members in a comment:** Now you can @ members and leave them comments in real-time. It is one of the better features for designers and developers to communicate efficiently.

- **Real-time notifications on project changes**

  - When the content of a project is modified, all project members will receive a notification in real-time.

  - You can upload huge images (like an image in 20,000 x 20,000 pixels) in mere seconds.

  - Your website or app images size is not all a concern, and you can upload and preview them in iDoc smoothly and quickly.

  - Handoff Designs with Auto & Manual Specs run in Mockplus iDoc seamlessly.

To collaborate and hand off design more seamlessly online, Mockplus iDoc provides "Flexible workflow" (which has three independent and customizable design steps in its "Design" module: Review, Comment, and Development).

The "Auto & Manual specs" feature is included in this "Flexible workflow."

More importantly, it is directly attached with the "Review" and "Development" steps in the "Design" module.

Designers can add specs manually for enhanced communication and handoff with developers.

Designers can add manual specs quickly to prepare simple PRD files for developers if the auto specs no longer explain everything.

Mockplus iDoc provides different kinds of manual markup tools to simplify the process, such as:

- **Text:** Designers will use the text tool to add any design information, such as the responsive interaction description, design illustration, design requirements, and more.

- **Coordinate Markup:** Designers can mark the coordinate information of any page location or element with one click with the assistance of the coordinate makeup tool. It will be beneficial when designers are required to add coordinate information for a floating button/element.

- **Spacing Markup:** Designers will draw a line around/between page elements with this spacing markup tool to add suitable spacing markups, like the word-spacing markups. Developers can see these spacing markups for implementing a web/app design as accurately as possible through this.

- **Color Markup:** Designers are free to click any position on a page with the assistance of this color markup to make the color value. It is also simple to mark up the color value of any element in a design asset.

- **Region Markup:** Developers will quickly check if designers are using this tool to add any page area's height and width markups.

Designers can easily and quickly customize text colors, background colors, line thickness/colors, opacity, and other markup properties easily and quickly to add more different specs in this "Review" part.

- **Development:** For making better and faster design, developers can check Auto & Manual specs.

Developers can also check the auto and manual specs according to their preferences in the "Development" part. They are free to show/hide the manual markups with one click if there comes any need.

Mockplus iDoc provides three spec viewing modes for developers in this part to enhance the work efficiency:

- **Not Selecting Any Layer:** Without selecting any layer, the specs will make you understand the distance between the layers as you move between them.

    Move between the layers, choose a layer, and hover over another layer to see the spacing specs between the two layers.

- **Select Multiple Layers:** Just hold the "Ctrl" key and pick multiple layers to know the distance between various layers.

Developers are free to check their desired design specs for better and fast design with the assistance of these modes.

User-Friendly Features to Enhance Your Design Process
Mockplus iDoc also provides more user-friendly features to improve your design process in the "Development" part:

- **Magnifier:** Users can view super spec details with the help of Magnifier with just a click.

- **Layer Tree:** Users will view the hierarchical relationships between page layers speedily to get familiar with the page layouts, even though the intuitive layer tree is placed in the left panel.

- **Layer Panel:** You have to double-click the location to open the layer panel to display all the layers if you have seen different layers in the exact location.

Whenever any requirement is necessary, you can disable a particular layer from this layered panel.

- **Spec Panel:** The comprehensive spec information will be shown in the top half of the spec property panel.

The displays of the spec codes are visible in the lower half of the spec property panel.
   Users will be able to copy the spec details and codes with one click simply.

Even though pixel specs are seen, you must hold the "Alt" key to show the percentage specs.

Mockplus iDoc can detect the nearest parent layers of the selected element as references of the percentage specs on its own, so you don't need to set anything in advance.

- **Switch Device Platform:** Switch the measurement units for multiple device platforms (such as the DP in Android, the rem for Web, and PT in iOS). If you want to customize the measurement, then it is also provided.

- **Auto & Manual Spec in Mockplus iDoc Step by Step:** We are going to provide you simple steps for you to use manual and auto specs in Mockplus iDoc:

  - Upload designs (including the PS/Sketch/Adobe XD files and images) to Mockplus iDoc.

  - Choose a page.

  - You want and click the "Design" module on the top navigation bar.

  - You will be able to use the page-turner or click the desired page on the left project tree if you need to change the selected page(no need to go back to the "Storyboard" module and select another page again).

  - You should add the desired specs manually in the "Review" step.

  - You have five markup tools to add manual specs: Text, Spacing markup, Coordinate markup, Color markup, and Region markup tools.

  - View manual and auto specs in the "Development" step.

When you have uploaded your designs to iDoc, the auto specs are automatically generated. The manual specs will be added in the "Review" step.

And you can be viewed both auto and manual specs in the "Development" step.

Developers will be able to download assets in multiple sizes, view spec details (including the text sizes, color opacity, and fonts), and export CSS codes with one click in this "Development" step.

But continuously increasing complexity of design makes design collaboration and handoff risky and time-consuming.

So you must get an effective tool to generate auto specs for your web/app designs. Generate all required information in just a few clicks and add manual specs to deliver every possible design detail to developers.

Mockplus iDoc is a perfect tool for you and your team to collaborate effortlessly and hand off designs with auto and manual specs online.

To own the Mockplus iDoc license, you have to pay an amount of $270.48. But you don't need to worry, you will get Mockplus iDoc with all the features for free if you follow the instructions given.

- Mockplus iDoc is a kind of web application that can work directly in your browser. You have to create an account to activate the subscription for free, no need to download it.

- Click HERE => Click to "Get Started For FREE" => Create a new account.

After successful registration, the Mockplus iDoc page will appear.

- Click to team name => Create team.

- Enter your team name => Click "OK."

- Open the Upgrade page, Enter license code: GSNW, and Click "Upgrade."

Enjoy!!

Pros

- You will be able to create and upload Axure/Mockplus RP prototypes quickly.

- You can create an online preview for your interactive prototypes in just one click.

- You can use a whole number of commenting styles for enhanced design explanations.

- You will be able to inform team members, track project status, and flexible workflow according to your preference

- Enhanced document management, backs up source files will be automatically backed up, and create historical versions.

- It will show you all pages in a single storyboard, which gives you a complete view of your designs.

Cons

- The prototype will be slow when it is tested on mobile.
- The Mockup needed to be permanently downloaded from the Internet.
- The logo of Mockplus will pop up when previewing the prototype.

Differentiator

Mockplus is a brilliant choice for designers, developers, and project managers to work together, show their talent, and create the best products online. It shows the preview of all the prototype pages at once.

Mobile Accessibility

You can easily access the software through devices such as tablets, laptops, and smartphones. It can also be available on both Android and iOS smartphones. The device supported by the software includes Windows, Cloud, and web-based. You can also download the app from the Play Store and App Store.

Support

- Online.
- Chat support.
- Phone support.
- Email support.
- Integrations.

Mockplus iDoc can be integrated with various applications and operating systems, including:

- Linux.
- Adobe Photoshop.
- Adobe XD.
- Sketch.

CHAPTER 3

Wireframing Tools

IN THIS CHAPTER

➢ Sketch

➢ Figma

➢ UXPin

➢ Axure RP

We have discussed Mockup tools in the previous chapter, and now we will discuss different kinds of wireframing tools in this chapter. The term Wireframe has a long history before the web design world adopted it. It was initially used in Computer-Aided Design (CAD) software to demonstrate an object's design with minor details requirements. The result was a kind of design that looked like it was made out of wires, then we ended up with wireframes. You can design a website service at the structural level with the help of Wireframe. It has a tremendous impact on your

DOI: 10.1201/b22860-3

content layout and functionality on a page, which empathically considers your needs and journeys. It had been used to make the fundamental structure before visual design and content were included.

WIREFRAMING IS ESSENTIAL IN UI DESIGN

A Wireframe is a kind of web page layout that establishes what kind of interface elements can be added to crucial pages. It is, in every sense, an inevitable element of the interaction design process.

The focus of a Wireframe is to give an early understanding of a visual page in a project to attain project team and stakeholder approval before the creative phase begins to set off. You will also be able to use a Wireframe to create the global and secondary navigation to make sure the terminology and structure used for the site attain the user's expectations.

A Wireframe Is Easier to Adapt

You can review and amend the structure of the key pages in a Wireframe format quickly. Iterating all the progress of the wireframes to a final version will give the design team and client the confidence that the page convincingly accommodates user preferences and requirements while fulfilling the critical project and business objectives.

Wireframing Is Used Early in the Project Lifecycle

Wireframes can be used at the onset of the design phase, even though it's used to complete the User-Centered Design process. To get user feedback before the creative process, a prototype usability test can test the Wireframe pages.

It has often been used to make an on-screen delivery using software like Microsoft's Visio, even though it can be hand-drawn simply. It is most convenient to create them in HTML if you use a Wireframe for a prototype usability test.

Advantages of Wireframing

You can review with your client in Wireframe as it provides an early visual. Users will also be provided to check it as an early feedback mechanism for prototype usability tests. It is not just a convenient to amend than concept design, and the designer will get absolute confidence once the client and the users approve.

From a practical perspective, the wireframes can ensure you position the page content and functionality correctly as per the business and the user's needs. This can be used as a good dialogue between members of the project team to agree on the project scope and vision as the project takes its course.

Wireframes can connect fundamental conceptual structures with the visual design of a site or app screen. Wireframes can be classified into the following three:

1. **Low Fidelity:** A less detailed early-stage drawing. These kinds of wireframes are usually hand-drawn sketches or shapes and lines representing an idea.

2. **Mid Fidelity:** show more component details can be shown in these wireframes. It focused on overall page structure and content layout.

3. **High Fidelity:** It provides more detail and higher level renderings of the components, with behavioral characteristics and a focus on the content layout as it's a later or posts iterative stage.

Wireframes in digital design have another user experience (UX) artifact and deliverable: the wire flow. It is a combination of wireframes and flowcharts, two artifacts that UX designers have converged into one for a purpose: to demonstrate and follow interactions that represent task flows in a product such as a web app.

Communicating the user journey is what designers encounter with wireframes. Wireframe map makes user journey smoothen even though there are enough complex ways of showing user journey.

A Wireframe map combines wireframes with user journeys (or user flows) to demonstrate the user's journey through a product using wireframes.

Disadvantages of Wireframing

It is always challenging for the client to grasp the concept as the wireframes do not include any design or account for technical implications. The designer needs to translate the wireframes into a design. So to support the Wireframe, communication is often required to elaborate why page elements are placed in such as they are. Not only that, it might initially be too much to fit within the Wireframe layout when content is added. So the copywriter and designer have to work closely to make this fit.

What Are Wireframe Tools?

Designers can quickly and effectively mock up an outline of a design through Wireframe tools.

You can drag and drop placeholders for headers, images, and content and quickly move them around to create a first draft that can be iterated on later.

What Makes a Good Wireframe Tool?

Technically speaking, you don't require a comprehensive Wireframe tool—a flowchart app is enough. But Wireframe tools outstanding functionalities will be much helpful for a website designer.

These include:

- **An uploadable or in-built user interface (UI) kit:** Basically, you have to select a Wireframe app. It will have an in-built UI component library or help you to upload your own to it.

- **Scalable Mockup fidelity:** Good Wireframe apps will allow you the free hand to scale between a stunning basic gray-scale low-fidelity Mockup and more graphically complex high-fidelity Mockups.

- **Collaborative working:** It is possible to share work digitally and let others make changes or leave feedback. It is an essential function in any Wireframe tool.

- **Export options:** Basically, you need to export sections of it as HTML or get access to basic CSS code once you've completed your Mockup so you can implement development more rapidly.

A. SKETCH

A Sketch is a vector-based tool used for mobile and desktop UI design, prototypes, and Mockups, and it has become an industry standard. This outstanding tool lets you edit and manipulate photos.

If you are a novice and have not seen a Sketch before, that doesn't hold you back from using Sketch as it is profoundly

user-friendly and will allow you to learn so quickly. It's solely for designers who want to cherish, not the layman cup of tea, and is suitable for teams providing client needs. It's intended for Mac users as its Mac-only app.

As a renowned design tool for UX/UI designers, Sketch allowed a platform for prototyping, vector editing, and collaboration. It included a growing library of hundreds of plugins that extend its functionality.

Wireframing in Sketch is almost the same as Adobe XD as it provides template/skits and drawing tools. You will be able to use Symbols excessively, which are reusable components. This can be defined once and used a lot of times (buttons, etc.). Instantiated Symbols can take on any changes made to the "master" Symbol. You inevitably have to make considerable changes throughout the wireframing process. So it will be one of the most valuable things to be mentioned.

Designers can create high-fidelity wireframes, Mockups, and Mockups. It is not a cloud-based app, and one of the main problems is that it only works with macOS.

Sketch has become one of the top vector graphics editors among designers in recent years.

As a Mac-only vector design program, its focus is on creating interactive app and web designs prototypes. Sketch's outstanding design working model enthuses your clients as it will provide an excellent feel for how everything looks and responds. That will help them give more practical feedback on the functionality (UI) and UX. So it lets informed approval in advance of the development stage, which will minimize any contentions that will save time and money.

Sketch mainly focused on collaborative design for screens, and it's relatively new to the fray. Other UX designs like Adobe XD (XD stands for Experience Design) introduced in 2016 as part of Adobe's Creative Cloud for Windows and Mac. It is also a vector-based tool.

A second vector-based competitor is Studio from the heavyweight Design System management platform, InVision. It has a built-in advanced animation module that is not available in Sketch and XD. the InVision platform lets you sync your work done in Sketch using their Craft Manager plugin.

Sketch provides multiple subscription models, costing $99 per year per device (either a mobile or computer), for individuals. This year of updates is also included in this model and Sketch Cloud (for online sharing and collaborating). You can renew for $69 per year to regain cloud benefits and regular updates. Getting volume licensing ranges from $64 per year per device for two to nine devices down to $49 each for 50 or more devices.

It would be mentioned that you will get only a single seat (for use on one computer only) when you purchase a license; you have to buy two seats if you are going to use multiple Macs, like a laptop and desktop. Many subscription-based apps often let two seats per license as a friendly act for hard-working creatives who work on their desktop at the office and on their laptops at home. A related inconvenience is that if you want to use Sketch on a new Mac or if you've had to reformat your drive, you need to unregister Sketch from your old machine/drive and then re-register.

Benefits of Sketch

- You can learn it quickly as its straightforward; intuitive interface.

- You will be able to create designs for multiple devices.

- If a client interacts with a laptop, desktop, phone, or tablet design, she can preview what would happen.

- Sketch Cloud syncing and sharing are helpful collaboration features.

- A collection of plugins can be used with Sketch (Craft, Abstract, Flinto, etc.).

- The toolbar is similar to Mac.

- Affordable.

When it comes to the benefits of Sketch, you can compare it with Photoshop. For example, you will work similarly to Photoshop, but it only consumes a lower price and can save your disk space. As a leading prototyping tool, Sketch has the instinct even to overtake photoshop at some point. The Sketch is much apt at screen design than Photoshop because it was explicitly designed for a new, more modern, purpose-built tool.

Sketch Basic Features

- Drawing, shape, and text tools.

- Edit shape points and Bezier curves.

- Arrangement operations (alignment, bring to front, distribution).

- Boolean tools (union, subtract, intersect, and difference).

- The Sketch is meant for prototyping, not for drawing.

  - **Define hotspots:** You can also assign areas of the screen as scrolling/non-scrolling and link and cross-link sections, instances, menus, pages, and Symbols. It is also possible to import text or images to populate the prototype with more realistic data than placeholders. If you are looking for designing with high-level precision, Sketch is spectacularly useful.

- It will provide tools for high-precision (grids and pixels grid, Smart Guides, rulers, etc.).

- Smart Guides will pop up before you set off your drawing for optimal precision.

- Holding "Alt" will help you to show the distance between the selected layer and others as well as between the layer and the artboard.

- Choose two layers and place them together.

- The Distribute Objects option helps you minimize distances between layers.

- You can set your layout grid.

- More Great Sketch Features.

- You can scale every property—radius, border, shadow/inner shadow, size with the scale tool.

- Pixel fitting helps you retain sharp pixels as you resize or align shapes.

- And colors are placed based on how often they're used as there are automatic detection of colors in your document.

- The color tool will help you to store your palette for a single document or globally.

- If you want more control over your colors, you can change RGB to HSB.

- Gradients are helpful for buttons, backgrounds, and icons.

- Use angular gradients for circular backgrounds and radial gradients for extensive backgrounds.

- You can make customizable background blur; all layers underneath the one selected will blur automatically.

- Text Styles allow you to reuse your preferred typography style across layers (set a global style).

- You can create reusable elements or Symbols to share across artboards; it will sync all the others if you are updated one. (If another team member updates a symbol, you can approve the update or detach it from your library.)

- You will be able to migrate from a library filled with icons and logos in Photoshop or Illustrator to Sketch.

- Auto-Save option will save your changes so you can work comfortably.

- The version history of your design also created by Auto-Save.

You have to work on an infinite canvas if you are first starting in Sketch. You will be able to customize the toolbar by right-clicking and setting your favorites by dragging.

A screen or an interaction within a screen is what an artboard demonstrates in Sketch. When creating an artboard, you can select from a list of standard screen sizes for iOS, Android, print, and web. It is pretty amusing that you are free to customize your own. An Artboard Manager plugin for OCD-level organization is also provided—you can snap your artboards into columns and rows to neaten them up.

A different kind of resolution or platform is represented in Pages in Sketch. You have to pull them all into a Page if you are going to create an artboard for iOS, and then you will be able to create another page for your Android design. A Sketch file can hold multiple pages and artboards. This helps you to access your workflow easily.

- Clicking on a layer helps you open up an inspector to the right, where you can change properties like most screen design tools.

- Simplicity is what defines a tool like Sketch. It's pretty amusing just how simple it is to navigate, even as a newcomer.

- It would be inconvenient to use photoshop tools for straightforward design jobs, so you can use something like Sketch as it saves your time and stress, and money.

- Its outstanding ability to reuse elements with ease, again and again, will help you save your time as a designer.

- Sketch's layout and vector drawing are robust and straightforward, so it's quite a pleasure to dive into it— even if you have too much more time experimenting.

The Sketch isn't a standalone app that requires extensive procedures to bring all your work together either; it facilitates almost seamless integration with the likes of Framer, Principle, and Marvel, which rarely leaves you wanting.

It's so wondering that Sketch is so cheap at a one-off payment of $99 (including free updates for a year).

Getting Started

A Sketch can be downloaded from the company's site (sketchapp.com); it will provide a 30-day free trial, which can be used with no credit card. It is a fact that MacOS 10.13.4 (High Sierra) or later version is only suitable for Sketch.

More powerful, RAM-loaded Macs are suitable if you use complex, multipage documents with hundreds of artboards.

Right on the download page, you will get Beginner's Guide, tutorials and tips, extensive documentation, and links to its social media and developer communities, chats, and blog, and Dribble. It's pretty scintillating that you would see a list of global design community events and meet-ups. Additionally, the site provides several free and premium Sketch App UX/UI resources, including mobile UI kits, Wireframe kits, Mockups, dashboards, templates, icons, and concepts.

Interface and Canvas

Sketch provides a clean, contextual UI with three main sections—and (by design) no floating panels. You will find the Sketch UI familiar if you are already a Mac user because it is modeled on the interfaces of Apple apps like Numbers, Pages, and Keynote. Apple's Dark Mode is also now supported in the latest version.

You can find the Page List with an inventory of your layers on the left side of the screen, individual content items on those artboards and layers, and the named content afterward. An Inspector in the right, and you can move the properties of the content on any layer you have chosen. Tools and actions are housed in the toolbar on the top. You can create the magic in center stage as it's your canvas.

A Page List lets you easily assign, organize, or change layers and allows your name, group, select, and duplicate content items. This process, in effect, makes your workflow exceedingly structured. You'll be in brilliantly excellent shape when it comes time to transfer files to a developer.

Sketch has an impeccable ability to smoothen your workflow by facilitating or automating common tasks with easy-to-make libraries, layer styles and text, Symbol instances, and presets. Not only that, to make things better and enhance Sketch's functionality in different ways, it provides hundreds of time-saving UI kits, templates, and plug-ins.

Artboards

Drawing and Typesetting in Sketch   The Sketch is all about prototyping. But you can draw in Sketch, and it's petty comfortable for that, but what's Sketch makes a stand out is its remarkable ability in prototyping. Even though it's worth getting an overview of what can be done with Sketch's drawing tools.

With just a click on the Insert dropdown, you will be able to set off all content creation, import, and assembly. There can find the expected shape, text, and drawing tools there. You can also find the arrangement operations like alignment, front, and distribution and non-destructive essential Boolean tools like Subtract, Union, Intersect, and Difference on the right. The intuitive and efficient vector tools allow creating and editing shapes, their points, and Bezier curves. The Sketch is not an Illustrator, and even it can have the ability to handle essential drawing tasks.

It would be better to add that typography in Sketch as it is straightforward and almost similar to Microsoft Word-like features. It provides various decorative options for fills, shadows, and borders. It would help if you had some manual effort in Sketch for making format blocks type as it doesn't support tabs—you have to use the space key to make your desired effect. That's just fine because any complex type-setting has any much helpful when designing responsive layouts. Everything is typographic (size, line hyphenation, breaks, and so on) changes when viewed on various devices.

Prototyping and Responsive Design

Sketch facilitates building an interactive prototype. You will be able to simulate the pathway of your site or app

(UI) and what the experience (UX) will be like, by assigning certain areas as scrolling or non-scrolling, by linking and cross-linking menus, sections, Symbols, pages, and instances, and define hotspots (clickable areas). It is imperative to note that you can freely use Sketch mirrors other than previewing your efforts within the app.

A new feature in Sketch is that you can populate prototype text and shape fields with dynamic, realistic data rather than being strapped to the usual Lorum Ipsum tedium. You are free to assign a source file from which you can import text or images to get selected text or shape layers.

The Sketch can be comfortably used as it delightedly play with others. It is not just applicable in-app only.

You will be able to copy and paste an icon created in Illustrator. Sketch made a grouped layer for your art after your import; you can use the icon and be added to a library or create a Symbol—it is almost like any art you made within the app.

Any properly devised, the screen-destined design must get its traction in today's market. This means that content within a web page or app screen auto-resizes and shifts, depending on the viewing device (laptop, mobile, desktop, and tablet). So, to make the best suit for each kind of device, the text resizes, line-breaks change, and images shrink, expand, or hide.

Sketch has to manually create variant layouts and simplify the different aspect ratios by copying and pasting each group or element. It would have been beneficial if there were a smart-adjust option. Because such kind of responsive layout modifications is like Responsive Resize in XD or even InDesign's Adjust Layout feature. It doesn't mean that Adjust Layout is an all-in-all tool to make a perfect solution, but it is absolutely a time saver and will give you a better place to begin than a blank page.

If you want to preview your Sketch designs in real time on your devices, you can use the complimentary Sketch Mirror for iOS and several apps for doing so on Android devices. But what is required, you need Wi-Fi or a USB connection to benefit anyone's workflow with much-informed design decisions and allow you to see your crops, adjustments, and text sizing live with Sketch Mirror on the actual device.

Output and Collaboration

You have different ways to share if you prepared your work for team collaboration and client feedback.

Uploading your document to Sketch Cloud is the primary method you can follow. After the upload, you get a URL. It will help you select someone to view the document and set one of three access levels: Download, Comment, or Use as Library. The built-in commenting tools can be used by anyone who has the link, and if they open the page on a phone or tablet, they will be able to preview the artboard(s) in full resolution so long as there is a layout for their device.

Sketch Library Preferences

Libraries provide you and your team to connect your project assets and presets. The Sketch helps you create these as it's pretty straightforward, and it's one best method of storing flexible brand assets in a single, globally accessible spot. It would be saved locally on your hard drive, on your server, or even in third-party cloud-based storehouses like Dropbox. A library is what you designate as it's just another Sketch page, which makes it available and handy for adding or revising assets.

You will get an alert about the update. A message will pop up in the screen's upper-right when you or anyone collaborating with you on the document edit a Symbol you created and return it to your design documents. You then choose to click to update, or you will be able to detach the artwork from the Library. The Sketch will show you a dialog window listing all your library components, the outdated symbol, and the updated Symbol side-by-side when you click on the alert. Sketch has the kind of tremendous ability to order and organize. It's fantastic to have complete information at your fingertips.

Alternatively, you can export artboards as PDF pages that can be marked up with comments in Apple Preview, Adobe Acrobat, or any other PDF-viewing software. Sketch also exports graphics, slices, and pages as JPG, PNG, and SVG files. What's more, it can ship code for SVGs and CSS attributes.

Creating Your Sketch Style Guide

It is possible to keep track of all the repeating elements for a project, from branding rules down to the amount of beveling for call-to-action buttons in a style guide. It is a comprehensive "living document." You can include anything from simple visual elements to vocabulary and approved imagery.

- **Step One: Organization:** To place Sketch files, plugins, and other necessary assets like iconography and fonts, you must create a master folder.

- **Step Two: Colors:** It is required to convert your colors into Symbols if you have already been selected color.

You have to squares of the exact size and change their colors accordingly for doing this. Click "Create Symbol" and store these elements using the color/ @color-name labeling system. color/@background-gray, or color/@FFFFF, Color/@pink are some examples of proper labels. Naming conventions are important. So you will get a format for everything which will adhere to from the onset.

- You have to add them to the style guide page when you have completed.

- You can save the color swatch in the documents section of your color palette.

T – text tool, R – rectangle tool, alt – measure distance can be used for helpful shortcuts.

- **Step Three: Icons:** Turning icons into dynamic symbols lets their color change comfortably to any colors saved in Step Two above. This means that after an icon is put into a design, you can change color through a simple dropdown menu, called an "override." It is possible by using the "Inspector" to the right of the canvas.

  You have to save the icon as a symbol. It would be better to make .svg for the asset type.

  You have to find the icon by going into the Symbol page and masking it with a default color from the colors you already saved. You have to overlay the color Symbol on top of the icon and click "Mask" in the toolbar. You can also use right-click and select "Mask" from the pop-up menu.

  After completing the masking icon, it is time to remove the fill by unchecking the checkbox under the "Fills" section in the Inspector.

It would be helpful to organize the icons in the style guide page and the same section to specify the color for active and inactive icons and other essential color specifications.

- **Step Four: Text Styles:** When selecting your fonts, you must specify Text Styles: H1, H2, H3, H4, H5, body, links, captions, labels, etc.

  Select the weight, size, character, and line spacing for as many styles as you need.

  If you want to reflect the style details selected, write out a word and format it. You can type anything automatically appears when you press T, the text tool.

  Then you have to click "Create new Text Style."

  You can organize the Text Styles on the style guide page.

- **Step Five: Assets:** Now, it is the time to combine all the steps you have taken to create some assets. It would be better to recreate assets if you already created them using icons, Text Styles, and colors. For example, You can see multiple colors of gray within the working design document that a design hasn't considered, so recreating the asset will ensure the chosen color's consistency. Don't forget to keep naming consistent, and you have to add assets to the style guide page as they are created.

  Some assets you can work on:

  - **Buttons:** You have to mask the button in the default color and remove the fill for making these dynamic symbols; just like the icons, you have to use the saved Text Styles if you want to keep the text centered at all times, spanning the width of the text box to be the same. It would ensure consistency.

These elements have to be saved as Symbols. You will be able to use the button/button-name naming system for this to happen.

You can use the override feature to change colors and labels.

- **Search Bars:** You need to apply resizing constraints to the search field and the icons and text used within the area.

  It is crucial applying text colors and styles previously saved in your document color palette.

  You need to save this element as a Symbol using search as the title. But it is crucial to adhere to the labeling system such as search/standard and search/no-icon if you have different types of search.

- **Radio Buttons and Checkboxes:** You can have a Symbol within a symbol, and one of the best ways to test it out is to create an intelligent radio button and checkbox assets.

  For making this happen, you have to make the button asset itself. You need to save this element as a Symbol using the checkbox/selected and checkbox/deselected as an example labeling.

  Now, it is the time for creating the input. You have to add placeholder text near the checkbox Symbol and then change all assets into a symbol. Because this is now an input, it is recommended to save the asset so that a good label would be input/checkbox/selected and input/checkbox/deselected.

- **Step Six: Use the Style Guide!:** It is a matter of fact that to make a project run more smoothly is an inevitable thing. If not, no such steps will help create a style guide. You have to apply the library to the document being designed if all the assets have been created. In Sketch, you will be able to go to "Preferences -> Add Library..." and add the library document.

  You will be able to access the library and its Symbols in the Symbols section if you've added a library to your project design file. You can see the iOS UI Design library with Sketch as a library option and the recently imported library.

  You can double-click on the Symbol itself if you want to update a symbol, and your library document will pop up. You have to go back to the design document and click the update button in the top right corner to make the changes.

  - **Bonus: Importing/Exporting Text Styles:** Text Styles can't be saved with a library; the Shared Text Styles plugin for Sketch solves this malice. You need to go to the library document and then to the menu upon you download the plugin: "Plugins -> Shared Text Styles -> Export..." you have to save this file in the same library document. Then, go to the menu again in your design document: "Plugins -> Shared Text Styles -> Import Text Styles..." and import the file you just saved. Your Text Styles will pop up.

  - **Bonus: Importing/Exporting Color Palettes:** Document colors are also not able to save over with a Sketch library as like Text Styles. Sketch

Palettes plugin can solve this puzzle. It is the same as above, and you have to export the palette using "Plugins -> Sketch Palette -> Document Colors -> Save Palette" and import it with "Plugins -> Sketch Palette -> Document Colors -> Load Palette." Don't forget to save it in the same folder as your other library documents.

- **Bonus: Fonts:** Craft by InVision is a suite of plugins that can achieve the next level in the Sketch. Craft lets you replace images with the prototype, stock photos, sync to InVision, create libraries, and more. Click "cmd-shift-c" in the document, and a stylesheet will generate if you download the craft. The fonts will be listed here.

Following the six steps discussed above will help large and small design projects work more efficiently, and the outcome will be enhanced. This style guide, Library, and UI kit can be used for one client, if they are unique or particular, or used for many projects if standard UI elements are recurrently created, such as prototypes and wireframes. It would be better to make these Sketch UI components properly as it will help you save a lot of time down the line and potentially across many projects.

Cons

- It is pretty buggy … even the latest v47.1 can be frustratingly so.

- Unexpected crashes and malfunctions of the app and supported plugins.

- It's Mac-only (sorry, PC users).

- The photo-editing capabilities are limited.
- Difficult to use with a Wacom tablet.

B. FIGMA

Figma has become a revolutionary graphics editing apps that transformed the design world profoundly. The better part of Figma is the fact that it's free to use. Figma was co-founded by Dylan Field in 2013 and got a $14 million Series A back in 2015. Dylan states that Figma wants to "do what Google Docs did for interface design for text editing in a TechCrunch article."[1]

It is one of the web-based graphics editing and UI design app. You will be able to do all sorts of graphic design work, from designing mobile app interfaces, wireframing websites, prototyping designs, crafting social media posts, and everything in between. When it comes to functionality and features, Figma has undoubtfully a close similarity with Sketch. But of course, its tremendous ability in team collaboration makes Figma distinct from any other such tools. Suppose you are in a profound puzzle about such outstanding capability of Figma. In that case, it's time to clear out all such confusion as we will explain how Figma will enhance your design process and is undoubtfully better than other programs at helping designers and teams work together smoothly.

You can work directly on your browser in Figma, which makes it different from other kinds of graphic editing tools. This will help you to access your projects from any platform or computer. So you can start designing without having to buy different licenses or install the software.

[1] https://techcrunch.com/2015/12/03/figma-vs-goliath/

Figma downloads

Why Is Web-Based a Good Thing?

- You don't need to download software, install it, and continually update.

- Your work will automatically be saved to a shared space in the cloud, so your files need not be saved or organized.

- One URL will be the source of truth that everyone can see. So you don't need to need to continually upload, sync, and arrange PNGs in multiple places.

Another reason why designers love this app is that Figma offers a generous free plan to create and store three active projects at a time. So it would be a better option for you to learn, experiment, and work on small projects.

Figma Works on Any Platform

Figma can work on any operating system. What you need is a web browser. Figma can be used in Windows PCs, Macs,

Linux machines, and even Chromebooks. You can expect only this design tool of its type to make this happen, and in shops that use hardware running multiple operating systems, which help everyone share, open, and edit Figma files.

Designers always use Macs, and developers use Windows PCs in many organizations. To make all of them come together, Figma helps a massive role. It also stops a different kind of PNG-pong (where updated images are bounced back and forth between design team disciplines). You don't need any mediating mechanism in Figma to make design work accessible to everyone.

Collaboration Is Simple and Familiar

Teams will be able to collaborate as Figma is a browser-based tool. You can see a circular avatar on the top of the app to view what others are viewing and editing in a file. Tracking is easy in Figma as each person in the team has a named cursor. You can see what others are viewing at that time by just clicking others' avatar zooms.

Real-time file collaboration lets you control design drifting. It is defined as either misinterpreting or straying from an agreed-upon design. You might have known that things like design drifting usually happen when an idea is conceived and implemented with much consultation while a project is taking its shape. This will, of course, often put upside down all of your established design, which in turn causes friction and re-work.

You can see what the team is designing in real time by simply opening a shared file through a design lead in Figma. This feature helps the design lead intervene, correct course, and save many hours that would have otherwise been wasted if a designer misinterpreted the brief or user story. This will not be available in another tool like Sketch.

Figma Uses Slack for Team Communication

Slack is used as a Figma communication channel. Whatever comments or design edits made in Figma are "slacked" to the team if a Figma channel is created in Slack; this functionality is unavoidable when designing live as changes to a Figma file will update every other instance where the file is embedded. It can then avoid potential disturbance. Changes to a Mockup are immediately vetted, even though it's required or not, and the feedback channel is live.

Figma Sharing Is Uncomplicated and Flexible

Figma lets permission-based sharing of any page, file, or frame (called an artboard in other design tools). If a member in a team is clicking on a shared link created to frame a page link, it will open a browser version of Figma, and a zoomed-in view of the frame is loaded.

Embedded Figma Files Provide Real-Time Updating

You can paste an iFrame in third-party tools as Figma shares live embed code snippets. That does mean if Confluence is used to display embedded Mockup files, those files are not "updated" by saving a Figma file as those embedded files will be the Figma file.

Any changes can be seen live in the embedded Confluence Mockup if a change is made to the Mockup by anyone in Figma.

Different kinds of tools were used to facilitate the exchange of design Mockups and updates before the inception of

Figma. So teams will be able to review and implement the current design as the iteration cycle was a series of back and forth file updates.

Third-party tools become redundant after the launch of Figma. But it's up to you to use all such tools if you are interested. Figma can handle the functionality of the third-party tools; as we mentioned earlier, you can make it possible to move from sketches to Figma. There is no "handoff" in the most rigid sense of the word.

Figma Is Great for Design Review Feedback

Figma provides In-app commenting in both design and prototyping modes, and the comment thread can be tracked in email or Slack. You don't need to publish PNG files or perform constant updates to get feedback from a team using a third-party tool like InVision or Marvel.

As team designers, you can discuss your work on a large screen, record comments, and fix issues during design reviews in Figma.

Developer Handoff Is Facilitated Using Figma

Figma displays code snippets on you can select any frame or object in CSS, iOS, or Android formats to use with the help of code snippets when reviewing a design file. Any developer can inspect these design components in any file they can view as there is no need for a third-party tool.

- If teams need to do more than simple measurement and CSS display, Figma will provide you full integration with Zeplin.

- Figma project files reside in one place—online.

- Figma can handle file organization by displaying projects and files in a dedicated view as an online app. It also provides your team with multiple pages per file, like Sketch, so

- Your efficient team can organize their projects accordingly:

- You need to create a project for the feature theme.

- It's imperative to make a file for an epic or significant feature.

- Then create pages in that file for each user story.

This is only one method of organizing files that could be made more or less granular, depending on the process demands.

Figma APIs Provide Third-Party Tool Integration

Figma lets proper integration with any browser-based app as now it has developer APIs. It will help integrate real-time displays of design files in their apps as most companies use this method.

There is a new add-on by JIRA to the Figma. It will allow developers, product owners, and quality engineers to continuously view the latest version of any Mockup from the designers.

Its API can fulfill customer requests for third-party plugins and feature enhancements that Sketch already provides.

File Versioning Is Automatic or On-Demand

Figma's built-in versioning system will allow you to mitigate any uncertainty surrounding updating live files. A designer will be able to make a named version and description of a

Figma file at any time; this can be done immediately after agreed changes are made to a design.

The only intentionally done changes to the original version will be affected the live file in the shared environment. Otherwise, it can't be affected. You can restore any automatically saved versions to make a duplicate or overwrite the original.

Prototyping in Figma Is Straightforward and Intuitive

Figma introduced a new tool that helps transitions between frames when Sketch recently added artboard to artboard prototyping. Its outstanding prototyping feature makes it unwarranted the need for another tool that does slideshow-style prototyping, such as Marvel or InVision. There's no need to export to review tools when you need only a simple presentation with transition.

Figma prototype will be able to dispense just like Figma design files; It is possible for anyone with link permission to view and comment on a prototype. Feedback can be captured in the tool's comment panel and recorded in Slack. It will see the design workflow, leave direct @messages for designers, and provide CSS attributes and measurements from inside the prototype.

Figma's Team Libraries Provide Ideal for Design Systems

Design Systems have become unavoidable for companies. So it's imperative for components (Symbols in Sketch and Illustrator) that are reusable, scalable, and "tokenized" for use in the pattern libraries available to UX designers and front-end developers.

Once a Figma team library is created, anyone with access to a project can use instances of the components in their designs if a Figma library is created. It will also be certain they are working with the latest versions.

It is easy to manage component libraries in Figma. Designers will create files full of components and can use on-page elements to make a pattern library. Every frame in a Figma page will become the organizational section in the team library.

You need to dedicate a project primarily to components to organize libraries. You can manage files within that project, and the pages within those files can be arranged accordingly.

Figma Is Built to Enhance Design Teamwork

The live collaboration tool of Figma will help you much in your design process. When building a Design System for several disciplines, it is essential to encourage full disclosure and keep a team on task, which profoundly helps you as a designer. Figma is easy for anyone to use on any platform and allows teams to quickly share their work and libraries.

Figma Can Be a Robust Design Tool for WordPress Sites

If you are going to build WordPress sites, Figma is an incredibly remarkable addition to the design tools which will help you make it happen. But you need to have professional WordPress development services to turn your Figma design into a fully functional website. You can convert the design into code in a simple way through the Figma: web developers can check, copy, and export CSS and design assets directly from Figma design files, which will reduce guess working and make handoffs effortless. Figma integrates multiple core features of other tools in one product to make it an enhanced and impactful workflow. It helps Figma to be an excellent tool to make corporate and other enterprise websites.

Easy to Share Files

If you use Figma as a web UX designing tool, it will take only a few minutes. You don't need to search through every conversation held with the client, and everything can be solved with just some clicks. This feature would be tremendously helpful if a developer asked to deliver some files to his clients on short notice. Figma can get it done in just five minutes, as it's quietly a time-saver, but you need to spend more time using a traditional process.

Numerous Plugins Available

Figma provides a number of useful plugins, so you don't need to search externally for plugins. Some of the best plugins are Iconify, Unsplash, Blobs Maker, Component Replacer, Remove BG, Content Reel, etc. We named only a few here, which is why web development companies select this software over others in the fast-moving market.

The Valuable Feature of Figma Mirror

When designing a website, you need to self-check as a web designer, as we are not infallible to be 100% perfect with our designs every time. This method of self-checking will also help us to make improvements. To analyze your work in the best suitable way, a feature of Figma Mirror will help you as a designing professional profoundly. You can figure out where improvement is warranted. So you can consult your client for her review. This outstanding feature will be a time-saver; our clients' money can be optimally utilized to provide enhanced quality.

Numerous Methods for Selections

It is essential to maintain a certain distance and place all elements on a website file. Figma provides different ways through which a user will be able to choose the distance she needs between the elements in the web prototypes. This method helps easily design a task for the developer as she can measure the gap between the items quickly and place them as needed.

Cons

- **You Can't Use Figma without an Active Internet Connection:** One of the main reasons why many people abstain from switching on to Figma is that it requires an active Internet connection all the time. You can't work without connecting to the Internet as this software is based on the cloud, so you need continuous connectivity.

- **Global Colors Are Absent:** For achieving flexibility, every website developing company has to invest much in colors as its essential component. Sadly, Figma provides no global colors in its module. It makes customizing a file more difficult. Global colors can enhance the performance of many systems in one attempt. There are added elements for multiple components that have not to be changed every time with any color change.

- **Searching Options not Available with Local Components:** It is a problematic option for freelancers as users will only search for a file uploaded into the team library. It is because freelancers always work solely and will not have a team of designers working together. That is not the case for a website development company as they have resources and a team. Figma would be a bad deal for a freelancer who doesn't need the features dedicated to an agile team.

- **Figma Need a High Amount of RAM and Decent Graphics Cards:** Figma works only in a system with above 4GB of RAM and a Graphics Card of high quality. This is not affordable demand that's a freelancer or low profile website designer can handle. Getting access to a website designed with Figma is not easy for all clients due to the mentioned above requirements.

Getting Started

- **Get Figma:** To start with Figma, you need to go to figma.com

  Then sign up and follow the instructions given. You can start with it after a minute.

  To quick start, you have to make a new file now anywhere from the menu or cmd+N. You are free to move the file later.

  You will not be able to store your files locally on your computer as it's a cloud-based. With the help of a browser, you will be able to access all your work from anywhere. It is not time-constrained, so you can also use it at any time.

One of the obstructions while working on Figma is connectivity as you need the Internet. But don't worry, you will be able to download the file to the app before you start your work offline.

• **Importing Old Sketch Files:** You can import Sketch files quickly and accurately in Figma. You just need to drop the Sketch file onto the Figma canvas. Done! You can find out all layers and setup in place.

One of the problems it faced was that it was impossible to copy and paste single items from Sketch to Figma. Even though it is possible, that can be converted into an image. So you had to import the whole file from Sketch even if you only wanted a single button. Now, that very problem has been solved; you can copy single items from Sketch if you right-click them and copy them as SVG.

• **Designing with Figma:** Setting up new frames(aka artboards).

You will be pretty familiar with this if you ever used the Sketch. If you need to see all frame options in the properties panel on the right-hand side, you need to press A or F, and you have to pick the size you want to work with or just draw your frame. You can work at actual pixel size as there is no quality loss when resizing in Figma. But it is still allowed to export assets any larger size you might be required.

You will be able to frame within each other in Figma. This option will provide you to make more complex designs that interact with each other.

- **Grid and Layout Columns:** You will be able to use a standard eight-point grid if you are using mobile. When it comes to web, it focuses more on layout grids (spacing is not of much importance), and so you will be able to start on the safe side with a popular 12-column bootstrap grid or a custom CSS Grid. It would be better to make a conversation with your developer beforehand and conclude which setup you will use.

  Now, it is time for adjusting the grid in the grid properties menu on the right-hand side. You are free to change from grid to rows or columns, make it fixed or fluid, and set margins and gutter as required.

  You can set up multiple grids and columns and store them in your styles is what makes Figma exceptional as its grids and columns are special to an extent. This is one of the most convenient features for adapting your layouts to various devices, sharing them with team members, or simply re-using them in other projects.

- **Layers and Groups:** You will be able to find the layers panel on the left-hand side.

  - **Layers:** You add create a layer in every new element automatically. It is possible to rearrange layers by drag and drop.

  - **Group Layers:** You need to group layers. You have to select layers and press cmd+G to keep your file organized for this making to happen. You can quickly move and copy those groups across frames with this. You need to press cmd and click on the item to select an element within a group.

- **Pages:** You will be able to set up different areas or sections of your design. No specific rule is mentioned on what or how to use them.

- **Assets:** All your components are stored here, and you can find your library button in this section.

- **Nested Frames** → In Figma, you will be able to nest frames in Figma. when it comes to structuring and prototyping, this would be pretty useful.

- **Vector Shapes:** For letting the creation of complex shapes, Figma uses something called Vector Networks.

  You need to select from the top menu or simply hit R(rectangle), L(line), or O(ellipse) and start drawing your shape for default shapes. Hold shift to keep proportions in place. Each shape automatically creates its layer.

  Hit P or select the pen from the top menu if you want to make your own, more complex shape. You have to press enter once you have completed the task. You don't need to connect and close paths. The properties menu on the right-hand side will help you to change properties and manipulate vector shapes at any moment during your design process.

- **Images:** You need to bring the image to your work area. It is time to adopt a new format if you are familiar with another tool like a Sketch.

  Images are always placed inside a shape in Figma. It is always like a mask. You need to go to Fill on the right-hand properties window and open the image properties if you want to change the behavior of the image.

In the dropdown, you can select:

- **Fill:** Image will fill the container.

- **Fit:** Your image will never be cropped or hidden when we resize it.

- **The Crop:** you need crop image to the size and selection. Here, you are only masking the image, so the rest of the image would not be lost as in the case of photoshop.

- **For the Tile:** You need to repeat the original images as it's essential and will be able to adjust the size of the tile.

Adjustment of properties such as saturation and color can be allowed in Figma. But you won't lose the original image properties at all as all of such are always re-adjustable.

- **Typography:** Figma has come into being with awesome Google fonts! You need to install the Desktop App or Font Helper for Figma to use local fonts. It is imperative to make sure that accessing the file has the same fonts installed by everyone.

  You need to press T to simply click or draw a text window and start typing. The right-hand side properties menu will allow setting all text properties.

  Text box behavior such as auto height, auto width, and fixed-size are relevant to note.

- **Styles:** Styles help you save and re-apply properties. You can update huge files in an instant this way. Styles can be created for text, color, effects, and grids such as shadows.

You need to click on the gray background next to the frame to see all used styles, and they will pop up in the properties menu on the right.

- **Create Color Styles:** Figma provides fabulous color and gradient styles as you will be able to set up one style and re-use it on text, fills, and outlines. You can change and delete style whenever you want during your design process by right-clicking onto the style.

  - Create and use a color style.

  - Create a shape.

  - You can change the fill to the color value.

  - You need to click on the square Symbol containing color styles.

  - Click on "+" to add the class. Done!

  - Create Text Styles.

  Text Style properties in Figma can only store the font family, line height, size, and spacing. This will help your styles library be neater and short as you don't require to duplicate a style for another alignment or color version of itself.

  - Setting up a Text Style works brilliantly as the same way with color styles:

  - To make it into a style, you need to click on the text you want.

    - You need to click the styles square icon.

    - Click on + on the right-hand properties menu and provide your style a name.

- If you need to add a style to an exciting text, click on the text and pick the style you need from the right hand menu via the styles square.

- You could change the properties or detach the style via the same menu if you added a style.

- **More Styles:** It is essential to add that grids can also be saved, shared, and re-used as styles in Figma. Furthermore, effects, such as inner shadow, drop shadow, layer blur, and background blur.

- **Components:** Components are UI elements, and you can re-used components across your design files. Components certainly play a significant role in making your design (and later programming) consistent and allow for easy updating and scaling. It will also save you a lot of work!

- **Creating Reusable Components:** You need to choose the object and press the create component button at the top of the screen or cmd+alt+K to create reusable components.

  You can see the purple component icon in the layer panel. You created a master component.

  If you need to copy this master component, it automatically creates an identical copy called an instance. All instances will be changed if we make any changes in the master components.

  Components in the Assets tab placed near Layers on the left-hand side can be seen and can also drag onto the frame.

- **Swapping and Nesting:** Master components will help you nest all instances of features inside. This means you can have components; it does mean, inside of components, you can have components.

If you use the right-hand side instance swapping menu or simply hold cmd+alt+option, you will swap nested instances. It will also allow you to drag and drop them from the assets overview or your team library.

- **Overwrites:** The master component is always followed in size and general layout by the instance, but you can change properties of the instance such as text, color, and outlines.

  Importantly, if you want to reset it to its original state, you can use the revert button in the right-hand properties menu. By using right-click on the instance, you can also detach an instance.

- **Naming Components:** You have to use "/" to name components, for example. Change "share-icon" to icon/ share as like Sketch. You can automatically create a parent category called icon with Figma, making swapping instances and exports a dream come true!

  If you have Master components on different pages, they will be organized by page.

- **Auto Layout:** Auto layout can create the creation of dynamic frames. It can grow or shrink if you alter the content within them; this is a significant milestone as it saves you tons of time re-adjusting and will let you check if your design works; keep going with actual content in one click.

- **Change Layers into Auto Layout:** Type your content If you want a new auto layout frame around the text layer with vertical and horizontal padding, shift+A will automatically help you create it. You can be take those values in the right-hand side auto-layout properties menu.

You can notice the button automatically resizing when you change the content.

- **Nested Auto Layout:** To compelling interface design, auto-layout frames will be nested, combining horizontal and vertical layout properties.

  The auto-layout frame can have a child frame inside a parent frame if you select the objects by clicking shift+A again.

  You will be able to select horizontal or vertical distribution and white space on the right-hand properties menu. You need to choose fixed with or height to prevent text frames from growing in one direction.

Prototyping in Figma

Figma provides outstanding prototyping for your app and web design.

Setting Up a Prototype

You need to choose a frame, and properties menu, and click on "Prototype" on the right-hand side. Pick the device you are designing for after clicking on "Prototype Settings." You have to choose the play button on the top right hand. Suppose you want to see your design in action. You can live Preview on your device if you download the Figma mirror app onto your phone.

Connecting Screens

It is imperative that on the right-hand side, yours, it's in the prototype menu. You need to be alert about how the selected element has a blue frame around it with a blue circle. You need to click and hold that circle. You can see a handle pop up, which can be connected with another frame if you drag.

You will be able to select the action (clicks, wipe, mouseover, etc.) in the properties panel on the right-hand side and the animation type (push in, move in, slide-out, etc.)

Overflow Behaviors

Figma provides other very realistic overflow behavior other than vertical scrolling.

- **Horizontal Scroll:** You need to choose all elements, group them, and draw a frame of the desired size copy or move the group inside, leaving the overflow hidden—select horizontal scrolling in the dropdown.

- **Panning Like Google Maps:** You need to draw a frame and add an image. Choose horizontal and vertical scrolling in the overflow behavior.

- **Fix Elements:** You need to "fix position" selected to make the header or button sticky (in Design > Constraints at the right-hand properties menu).

A smart animate will look for matching layers to recognize differences and animate layers between frames in a prototype. This allows you to create powerful prototypes.

Sharing and Working with Others

Presentation Mode

If you want to open the presentation screen on a new tab, press the play icon on the top right corner of your menu. This will allow you to click through all frames. All prototyping will be added, and it will add a device for mobile design. It will provide comment and full-screen mode, as well as an easy sharing link.

Create a Team and Project

Teams on Figma, let's collaborate with others or structure your work. You will be able to add projects, invite members, and store-specific libraries.

You need to click the "create team" button on your Figma to create a team, overview, and follow the instructions. Your teams will become more powerful with different payment plans.

- **Team:** A team of people, e.g., developer, designer, copywriter, etc.

- **Projects:** To keep related files together.

- **Files:** Single design files the actual design happens here.

Library

One particular place holding the latest update of all components and styles must be needed when working in a team that will help all team members access—a so-called single source of truth. The Figma team library provides this brilliantly well, and it will be the backbone of your Design System.

You will be able to publish color styles only to the team library with the free plan. You are required to get a Pro plan to save components.

- **Create Team Library:**

  - You need to go to Assets and click on the book icon on the left-hand menu.

  - Press publish.

  - You need to give a name to your publish; this can save a copy (version control fundamentally).

  - Open a new file within the team.

  - You need to click on the library icon in the Asset tab and activate the library you just created. Done!

- **Update Team Library:** When changing a master style or component, Figma will force you to update the team library. All other team members will get a notification that updates are available once you have done your update; they can review and update single components or update everything in one go.

Sharing with Other Designers and Developers
You need to click the blue share button in the top menu and enter an email address or copy the link and send it to invite people.

Other copywriters and designers → Set to EDIT MODE. It will provide access to all features. You can see other users' cursors and avatars and work alongside them in real time in the same file!

Developers → Set to VIEW MODE. This will show them all specs (iOS, toggle CSS, and Android code). They can also access your prototype in action and can download any assets in size required.

Exporting Assets

As described above, in Figma, all assets can be exported in any size directly from the shared files, even if only rights to "view" are granted; therefore, as a Designer, you don't need to export anything yourself. If you, however, would like to, in any case, this is how it works:

- Choose the object.

- Click on Export on the right-hand side properties menu.

- Define how to export and done!

C. UXPin

UXPin helps your design meets code and makes your prototypes come to life.

UXPin is a code-based design tool that merges engineering and design into one unified process. It is possible to build prototypes that feel real because of variables, state-based animations, conditional interactions, and strong expressions. It does mean UXPin will let you prototype anything on the web accurately. This web-based design tool is somewhat different from others that you may have been familiarized with. It is an end-to-end UX platform. It is not merely used for just a screen or page design but focuses on creating Design Systems.

When other tools lay focus on User Interaction, UX emphasizes user experience, which helps to create new

experiences altogether. It is to be noted that even though a single person can use it, the UXPin material design UI kit will also be used for larger teams of designers.

UXPin lets create designs from the conceptualization stage to testing and development while maintaining design consistency all around. UXPin allows robust and credible understanding between designers, developers, engineers, and other stakeholders involved in the project. It has tremendous ability to enable multiple users to lean in on the work process.

The UXPin UI kit will provide you with several items, interactions, variables, elements, and expressions. The most valuable thing is its ability to transfer the items into HTML code and real interaction, which in turn lets you save your precious time. UXPin is secure, fast, and a cross-collaborative tool to create designs for any screen-based digital solution or product.

UXPin will meet all your design needs, no matter whether it is simple or complex digital solutions. This software allows you to leverage specific requirements that require some intricate work.

UXPin provides native desktop apps available for both Windows and macOS devices as well as its web-based version.

Rapid Prototyping

When it comes to speed, UXPin renders you thousands of ready responsive components for iOS, Bootstrap, Material Design, as well as some big sets of icons ready to drag and drop into your design. It will provide you with a nice set of animations that you can select from and your interactions and transitions if you need more.

Interface Design

UXPin lets you have several rooms for customization, even though there are libraries that profoundly help you put together a working prototype quickly. By applying drag-and-drop integration, you can create your animations or use your Sketch and Photoshop files.

Hi-Fi Prototypes

Even though it had beneficial libraries for quickly assembling a working prototype, UXPin still lets you have a lot of room for customization. You can create your animations; It can allow you to add audio and video and create your animations to make your prototypes exceptionally better, just like the final product.

Creating states will be better for advanced prototyping. There are sets of items, like buttons, boxes, and images clubbed as components in UXPin that will help to change between configurations after the interaction. For instance, two configurations—states—each would show different states of a button. You need to click the element first, then toss between the states.

Creating different states is relatively straightforward. It is possible to move elements within a state if you are viewing a particular state. You have to change their styles like opacity and color. You are allowed to give them interactions or mask them altogether.

Code Snippets and Use Cases

It is possible to add custom code snippets to any element while prototyping. The code will come along for contextual documentation when you intend to re-use.

To make it more obvious, you are free to use contextual documentation to add descriptions of use cases (or whatever other notes you need to attach to elements). It would not be much helpful as the code snippets but will not make any obstruction to over-communicate.

Collaboration and Handoffs

You might have known that each team member is unique, and it will reflect on their output. They all possess very specialized skills, so we often stagger to maintain the macro perspective required to build a fine product. That problem might change completely with real-time collaboration.

Members will co-design in real time with automated notifications for updates and new comments as per the permission you set for the team. Anyone with a preview link can be read the documentation kept within the actual prototype. Going back and forth, everything from the planning table to designing will be streamlined as the comments turn into contextual feedback that can be immediately acted upon.

Prototype Documentation

It lets you write down any notes for technical nuances and edge cases when you prototype. Very impactful for complex enterprise products.

Specs, Assets, and Code

To auto-generate specifications, we have to change to specs (typefaces, colors, etc.) and CSS code for the final developer handoff. A handy workflow is required to import your file into UXPin, transform the static design into a prototype, then enter Spec Mode for developer handoff if you are using Sketch.

Comment on the prototype will be allowed to different team members at the time of Preview.

Scalable Design Systems

When rapidly scaling your product (adding cross-platform compatibility, rolling out new features), you may get annoyed to get caught in a cycle of redundant work. But it would be helpful to use the Design System Libraries and Symbols features to create a reusable toolkit.

Of course, you may take time to build your library initially, but you can save much in the long run.

Design System Libraries

Team pattern libraries improve the consistency of design and make component-based design a simple matter of dragging and dropping the right elements. There's no need to refer to a separate style guide; the elements you are working with are your style guide.

Because they live in the cloud, the Symbols in the Design System Libraries in UXPin behave like a more collaborative and consistent version of Symbols in Sketch.

To start building your library, right-click on any element, then click "Add to Library."

Once you've built out the library, you can review all the elements in the Design System Library itself.

Components

Components are an exceptionally nifty feature that makes you modify an element just once and automatically update it for your entire product. If you know Adobe Photoshop, this is like "Smart Objects" in Photoshop: Very powerful.

UXPin Merge

Users will be able to import and keep in sync coded React.js components from GIT repositories to the UXPin Editor with the help of Merge. The components used by developers during the process of development are identical to the imported components. Components will look, feel, and function (interactions, data) like the real product experienced by the end users.

- Merge designers will be able to use components in the code repository without any extra work or expertise in the coding.

- No need for redrawing elements that have already been coded.

- They can test advanced use cases with interactions and data available in production code.

- Because the components used by the designers have already been coded, engineers can enhance their workflows.

- They can use auto-generated specifications for every design that refers to the composed, real JSX.

- It is possible to be a part of the advanced prototyping process by writing custom components, iterating on code, and connecting components to data sources.

- Design ops/Design Systems teams can build unified Design Systems serving both engineers and designers from a single source of truth set up in code.

- It is essential to control changes to components in the system by controlling properties of React.js components (flow or typescript types prop-types and interfaces).

- The version of the Design System has to control and required coordinate releases via GitHub for both engineers and designers.

- Engineering and design leaders will be able to connect and synchronize engineering and designing processes.

- To understand the agile process without a waterfall handoff.

It is crucial to benefit from the shorter path to testing ideas and delivering new products/features to the market.

How Does It Work?

The paradigm that the UXPin paradigm has been created helps it to merge. UXPin has been a code-based design tool from its very inception.

Most design tools on the market (Sketch, Photoshop, InVision Figma, Studio, etc.) are built on the image-based design tool paradigm.

If a user draws something on the canvas or an artboard, the tool provides raster or vector graphics in this paradigm. Later, you will be able to give full-page images in JPEG, PNG, and SVG. This kind of file format is unlikely to enable importing interactive components and exporting fully interactive prototypes. It is not easy to relate to the way developers work and always look different from what can be achieved with web technologies in a browser; this will indubitably cause a significant disconnection between engineers and designers.

If a user draws something on the canvas in the code-based design tooling paradigm (UXPin), then the tool creates the HTML/CSS/js code and provides it visually with the assistance of the browser rendering engine.

You will be able to give any code that the browser can render inside our design editor with the help of this. This capability leaves behind image-based tools and gives us a technological advantage over them.

Merge Technology works in multiple steps to complete its goal:

- Merge analyzes and serializes (creates a data structure representing the repository) the repository where coded components are stored.

- Merge uses provided webpack config to build all the components.

- Merge ships all the data to UXPin and provides coded components in a Design Systems Library.

Learn UXPin

You are eagerly want to start but perplexed; where to start? You can be creating and managing team libraries to share information between screens with these examples!

- Creating and using Libraries in UXPin.

- Scrollable content.

- Pop-up.

- Adding videos and sounds.

- Simple navigation.

- Sharing information between screens.

- Minimum technical requirements.

You must have the following requirement to use the UXPin desktop app.

- macOS Sierra or later will only be allowed on macOS devices.

- Windows 10 in a 64-bit environment is required on Windows devices.

- Browser: Google Chrome, Apple Safari, and Mozilla Firefox.

Tip

It would be better to use the latest version of Google Chrome in the first place itself to ensure a good experience.

You can use Apple Safari or Mozilla Firefox on the preview. It is crucial to be sure about a stable Internet connection. The UXPin performance might get affected if you use different browser add-ons and plugins. So it would be better to disable them for UXPin.

Using UXPin on Mobile

You will use your prototypes on mobile devices (Android and iOS) in the UXPin Mirror app. The prototype on your mobile device will also update quickly as you make changes in the editor.

Supported Versions

- iOS 10 or later.

- Android 5.0 or later.

You can download the app from App Store or Google Play.

Working on Multiple Devices

You are allowed to be logged in two devices at a time if you are using UXPin on more than one computer. You can work in the browser from one and one with an open desktop app.

Working Offline

It doesn't make any problem if you are offline, as it will allow you to continue editing the currently open page in the UXPin desktop app. However, you need to remember that some things might not work in such a situation. You need to keep the desktop app and the browser open until the Internet connection is returned, which is when your changes will be synced automatically.

How to Create a Prototype in UXPin?

Now, we are going to create a simple prototype with the UXPin UI kit. It is important to note that you may not get an option to choose a dedicated platform for the designing purpose with UXPin. You can only select between importing an existing one from Sketch and other UXPin alternative tools or a new project with this.

- **Step One:** When you select the blank document from the dashboard, the artboard will open up, which will help you to make your design as per the requirements. Wait! You need to identify the screen size of the platform on which your website or application will run before the beginning.

    You will not get an option to select premade platform-specific artboards in UXPin; you have to make your size. There are detailed dimensions visible on every element, figure, drawing visible on the right-side panel.

    You can choose the needed elements from the sidebar panel, which allows you to add shapes, figures, video, images, audio, forms, text, and various other necessary items for the prototype.

    You will create any form or shape with a pencil or pen and refine it before finalizing the design.

- **Step Two:** You need to add the elements like an image upon adding the needful text and setting its typography. It will provide you to import any image you need from your device to the design and set its size according to the design.

    This is what makes the UXPin UI kit exceptional, as it lets free hand drag the cursor to fit the image into the design contrast to adding the original sized image and then editing its size.

You can also set the image at the entire screen's background by using the opacity function and putting it at any other place you want.

- **Step Three:** The UXPin material design UI kit provides you with the most used buttons and other elements required for the design. So you will be able to select the category of icons from the dropdown menu and insert the right design.

  Click the Preview button to check out how it looks on the screen when your design is ready. However, you may not get the same UX due to the absence of an underlying device.

  However, you can share the design with the other team members and clients. You can let the clients or users add comments and view the design specifications for easy handoff or any kind of UXPin alternative.

- **Step Four:** In the last step, you will also add interactions that will act like a transitioning sequence from one page or screen to another.

  You can set an interaction on medical records from this screen. Users will enter on the second page, i.e., medical record, once they click on the circle made in front of the text.

  After making a design, you will realize that there are a few things that every user wished that the UXPin UI kit should, and some other elements must have been made more smooth and easy to access.

Pros

- Improved design consistency thanks to Design System Libraries and Symbols.

- Creative freedom in design and prototyping with lo-fi and hi-fi capabilities.

- Intuitive comment tracking, design approvals, and project tracking.

- Sketch, Google Fonts, and Slack integrations.

- No redlining and minimal documentation are needed, thanks to Spec Mode.

Cons

- Slight learning curve.

- No birds-eye view of prototype screens.

- No Illustrator integration.

D. AXURE

Axure RP is a robust design tool for creating highly interactive HTML prototypes for mobile, web, and desktop application projects. Rapid prototyping is the main focus of the tool. Axure RP is an on-premise application development platform that lets users prototype and Wireframe software projects. It helps non-technical businesses to publish diagrams and prototypes in the Cloud or on-premise platforms and demonstrate designs for clients.

Axure RP's features comprise Sketch, wireframe, flow diagrams, prototyping, notes, Axure share publishing, co-authoring, revision history, team project hosting, SAML-based single sign-on, author and reviewer accounts, and workspace access management. The platform's diagramming and documentation tools are used to create and manage flowcharts, wireframes, Mockups, user journeys, personas, and idea boards. Additionally, Axure RP comes with built-in and custom libraries, which enable users to enhance and style diagrams with fills, gradients, lines, and text formatting.

Axure RP comes with AxShare App for iOS and Android platforms, which provide interactive view possible to types on smartphones and tablets. It is a handy tool, and you will be able to use it for prototyping, wireframing, and creating specifications, commonly used. Axure RP is always used by business analysts, UX designers, information architects, user researchers, and product managers to websites and design applications. It is possible to quickly prototype, then visually present your website or application without writing a single line of code.

Axure lets users quickly create prototypes and wireframes from any rough ideas they may have.

What Can You Create in Axure RP?

It will help you to use it in the Design and Research phases of a project.

Some of the deliverables you will be able to create in Axure RP during the Research phase.

- **Sitemaps:** A site totally for architecture.

- **Personas:** It is all about target user needs and pain points.

- **User Workflows:** Need to go through a specific set of steps to complete a task.

- **Customer Journey Maps:** All the pain points, touchpoints, and opportunities your customer go through when using your service.

Following are some of the deliverables you can create in Axure RP during the design phase.

- Wireframes help you to create the structural layout of content and functionality of a mobile app or website.

- Prototypes are used for Interactive wireframes.

- Specification document allows you to share the document with the developer detailing the scope of design work.

- You will be able to found out links to these downloadable free and premium Axure templates at Humbleux.

- You will be able to achieve a very high level of fidelity/detail based on what you'd like to convey and how much time you can invest in a project.

It is, of course, one of the powerful tools to tell and present the entire story of how you as a designer got to a solution for your team or the client.

Is Axure RP Easy to Learn?

When you make up your to learn Axure RP, you may get confused about its functioning.

But it is pretty straightforward to use the Axure RP interface.

It is almost like most prototyping and animation programs; the Axure RP learner curve also makes the interactions you need.

First of all, let's make clear the Axure RP interface.

The company started in 2003, and now they introduced a new version, 10, which can be run on both Windows and Mac.

Almost like any other design tool in the market, it also has a straightforward interface.

Axure RP 9 Interface

- It contains specific device boards, formatting tools, central canvas, layers, and a page hierarchy.

- You will be able to quite simply drag and drop onto the canvas with the help of a library of widgets.

- It will help your process of designing quite quickly and straightforward.

- Different kinds of application states will be stored in the Interaction section, which will help you make your prototype alive.

- This allows you to create an HTML prototype to be viewed in your default browser when it is published or previewed. The interactions will be turned into JavaScript and your formatting and styling into CSS. It helps your prototype to run on both your mobile devices and desktop.

Pretty cool.

It is possible to share with clients or the team to review and comment on your designs through a public link provided by Axure.

Is Axure RP Suitable for You?

Take a look at the users currently using Axure RP:

- Web designers.

- UX designers.

- UX consultants/analysts.

- UX researchers.

- Senior/Head designers managing teams.

- Students.

- Lecturers.

It would not be a better option for a UI designer.

Axure RP is always a prototyping tool that helps your UX activities, not a predesign tool like Adobe XD, Sketch, and Figma.

So it is hard to find union operations, masking, or an emphasis on Design Systems.

Not only that, vector functionality was added to the Axure in its eighth version.

Some tools in Axure Rp are pretty well, so they will help you with particular tasks. It would be good for you if you were a UX designer.

Axure RP is an irreparable tool for UX-related functions, and it's used profoundly in the concerned fields.

Its highly impactful focus on function over form help Axure RP to become a standard in the UX industry. This specificity lets the UX professionals focus on layout, strategy, and functionality.

This doesn't mean that it is hard to make a scintillating interface with Axure; choices are abundant to do that job with another tool.

Is Axure RP Worth Buying?

It will be worth it if you use Axure RP to play out your ideas professionally to share with a team or present to a client.

The company is constantly enhancing the interface, which will undoubtedly create new ways of using the tool.

How Much Is Axure RP?

You have to pay $29 per month.

- Unlimited reviewers.
- Unlimited prototypes.

- 1,000 projects on Cloud.

- Advanced prototyping

- Wireframes, Diagrams, and Documentation.

Axure RP enterprise versions and collaboration functionality require another pricing pattern.

It is possible to use the 30-day trial version to get a feel of the program if you are a newcomer or want a low budget.

"You will get it for free if you are a student."

Try to see if you can do a project with it.

And then create a proposal motivating your company to purchase it.

When we consider the Price pattern, it's a worthwhile investment in the long run, and Axure has a massive community, so you can get advice when you get stuck and with Axure RP, you will be able to do the following.

- You can help your clients to visualize design concepts.

- You can give interactive, transparent, visual prototypes to development teams to build a product, application, or web.

- UX researchers can test design ideas before spending money on development with the help of it.

- Allow business analysts to create entity-relationship diagrams (ERDs) and flowcharts and for business analysts.

- A prototype can be enhanced with amazing animations.

- With dynamic panels, you can create an effective prototype.

- The repeaters concept can be used to create dynamic grids.

- Adaptive views and conditional statements will help you make high sophistication to your prototypes.

- In Axure, you can communicate your design ideas with a robust set of tools. It will allow you to make your designs spectacularly.

Axure created this tool specifically to help UX designers to create rapid prototypes; Axure RP is a robust design tool for creating highly interactive HTML prototypes for mobile, web, and desktop application projects. Rapid prototyping in the Axure RP is the main focus of the device. Axure RP is an on-premise application development platform that lets users create prototype and Wireframe software projects. It helps non-technical businesses to publish diagrams and prototypes in Cloud or on-premise platforms and demonstrate designs for clients.

Axure is an outstanding application. UX designers can create rapid prototypes with this Axure tool called Axure UX. It will allow you to create a quickly constructed, rough prototype mainly to present an idea as early as possible in a design process. But it is to be noted that you can also create very high-fidelity prototypes, enabling UX researchers to test their prototype with users in real time if it is warranted. It will indubitably let you share design ideas with a set of tools and make your project worthy.

Its online help services make Axure more popular, and it has a tremendous ability to evolve and get updated with more robust versions.

Create a Prototype with Axure RP

Axure is one of the excellent prototyping tools to date. It provides outstanding features like resizing, drag and drop, and many similar options. You will be able to create highly interactive designs in Axure. Its quite profound choice of rapid prototyping makes your creativity fast deliverable to the clients. Collaboration between the engineers is also allowed with the help of a quick and shareable portable file format. You will get responsive and adaptive designs. It will provide you with multiple widgets and templates that can be customized according to your wishes and possible to use in another project.

Following are some of the Axure mobile prototype examples. You can export the screen from Omnigraffle as PNGs. You can crop and mask it, and it will be possible to add layers. It will also allow you to add Interactive components such as drop-down menus and form fields and create a functional prototype quickly. When we consider desktops, prototypes for mobiles are different. You can customize Azure mobile prototype options. It will allow you to provide the device screen details such as length, width, and pixels.

To allow you to create an attractive prototype, Axure introduced different features.

You can add Pages in the Axure Prototyping Tool.

- **Pages:** First, you need to open a new RP file. When you hit the "Add Page" button on the right-top of the screen, pages will be added. Suppose you want to edit the page; you need to open it on a canvas by double-clicking on the page.

- **Canvas:** If you want to build your design by adding boundaries and setting the dimension of your pages in line with the device you are working on, the canvas will help you make it possible.

- **Widgets:** Widgets will allow you to add the design or prototype that you are building. A pre-installed widgets library is provided in Axure, and you also get Flow, Default, Sample UI Icons, and patterns. You can add creations libraries created by your teammates.

- **Interaction:** To make the prototype more engaging, you can add Interactive elements to the prototype to make it more attractive. It will be possible by adding a link to another page.

To make it happen, you need to adhere to the following rules.

- **Step One: "Pages add a new page in the pane."** Now, it is the time to add two pages, page 1 and page 2.

  On page 1, you need to drag a widget on the canvas from the library's pane.

  Now, the time has reached to select the button and hit Click or Tap > Open Link in the > interaction pane.

When you see the second page on your screen, you need to select it and click OK.

A Preview button can be seen on the top right of the UI. So you have to click on them to open the prototype in your browser.

Click the button to visit page 2.

- **Step Two: "Hiding and Showing Widgets for Your Axure Prototype."** If you want to open on the canvas, you need to open the new PR file and double click on page 1 in the pages pane.

  You need to drag three buttons and the placeholder widgets on the canvas from the library's pane.

  The text of the button needed to change and set to Show, Hide, and Toggle.

  You need to click the placeholder to hide it and click the Hidden icon in the Style pane of the style toolbar.

- **Step Three: Sharing Your Axure App Prototype:** It is possible to share it with your teammates or publish it to the cloud for free after you are done with your prototype. For that, you need to click the Share button at the top right of the screen and enter your project name and password into the system. After that, hit the publish button for the shareable link of your completed project.

CHAPTER 4

Appraisal

This fast-moving world forces us to progress speedily and recapitulate our very ideas as efficiently as possible. So it's an irresistible fact that Building Mockups make a convincing balance between true-life representation of the end product and ease of modification. Mockups are much helpful both for the creative phase of the project and the production phase, which let you represent the target product.

Making Mockups a part of your development and creative process lets you speedily and easily ideate and iterate on your site before you've invested in the actual coding process. You'll have something tangible to show potential clients or a helpful reference to work from when you start moving forward.

We have comprehensively covered the very idea of Mockup and why it has become an irreplaceable stone of your mesmerizing creativity in Chapter 1. It is a static web page or application design that attributes many of its

DOI: 10.1201/b22860-4

final design components, but it may not be functional. A Mockup is not precisely accessorized as a live page and permanently houses some placeholder data.

As a "static design." the functionality of a live website is not included in a Mockup. Even though a Mockup would consist of a colored CTA button, as an example, it would not pop up a form when clicked on, unlike a website or the prototype of a website. A Mockup may sometimes light up a cover image at the top of the page, but it is unlikely to have an active carousel like a website.

You are familiarized that a Mockup is not the first stage of website development, so it's on its way to being a completed product, but it still has a ways to go. A Mockup may contain placeholder copy or images, but it is meant to provide an excellent feeling of the page, though not what it will act like.

In a comprehensive analysis, we have meticulously waded through the purposes of Mockups as it serves as a visual draft of a web application or page. It has constantly been evolved to bring life to an idea or Wireframe and let a designer examine how different visual elements can work together.

A Mockup is a kind of visual presentation of a website or app. Designers always use Mockups to highlight their website's layout and functionality to their prospective clients.

While Wireframes and prototypes are low-fidelity (low-fi) formats, Mockups are more intuitive. They help clients visualize how the final product will look, feel, and work.

Mockups also help remove ambiguity regarding the client's expectations. Clients can detect gaps on the website by looking at its Mockup and suggesting early product revisions. By using Mockups for each iteration, designers can create a final product that meets client requirements.

This means a Mockup can make or break your website.

It will allow stakeholders to examine what that page will look like while pointing valuable suggestions for appropriate changes in color, images, style, layout, and more. If you are curious about a page using a secondary color, you can examine how that will pop up by creating a second version of the Mockup. Likewise, if you need to make any change, like inserting a header while centering an image, your Mockup will let the team watch how that specific change might look.

A page needs to be created for a particular purpose with a determined goal in mind. Mockups allow the team to see how that purpose can be attained through the layout developed by a user interface (UI) designer with a Wireframe and how that layout can become a reality using their visual creativity and brand standard.

You might have learned from the ebook about where a Mockup comes into the web design process. Yes, when it comes to stages, Mockups come at approximately the midpoint of the web design process, and when it comes to time, they're still in the early stages of design.

It is also noted here that we also come across in Chapter 1 about Wireframes. Wireframing is an avoidable part of the design process. Throughout a mobile app or website project, you will have a lot of ideas, and the best way to determine those ideas is to brainstorm. This Wireframes brainstorm's main intention is to make them with minimal effort, as to facilitate creativity. It doesn't matter whether you are a designer; wireframing is a necessary skill to have in your toolkit. It's conducive for marketers, product managers, or anyone else with ideas for a mobile app or website. It is an irreparable tool for visualizing user experiences (UX), iterating on ideas, and sharing ideas with others. It is undoubtfully performed like a design blueprint. They stipulate a path for conceptual structuring out an application, whether structurally or visually. It will help you in communicating the following points:

- Content will allow you to know.

- The contents are displayed on the page.

- The structure will allow the pieces of the application to fit together.

- Information hierarchy allows you how are the information organized and displayed together.

- Functionality is all about the interface's work.

- The behavior will allow the user to interact with the interface and how does it behave.

- The Wireframe is a framework or skeletal blueprint that outlines a UI's functions and basic design (such as an application or website).

Wireframe help you to communicate quickly and easily communicate:

- The contents of the page

- The page structure and layout

- The app's functions

The purpose of Wireframes may change with the people using or creating them. It will allow you to convey the information we want others to know, whether we hand sketch it or prototype it to take the product's clear vision.

The wireframing stage is about creating a rough layout for the page, taking a goal or an idea, and using design theory to create a page that will achieve that goal. The Mockup is often used to take that layout and make it more flexible and lifelike.

After stakeholders reach an agreement on the visual aspects of the Mockup, it goes into the Prototyping stage, where actual development is required to turn a Mockup into an almost near-functional version of the page. Indeed, all of this happens before a page goes live and is tested with real users or visitors.

A Wireframe is a kind of web page layout that establishes what kind of interface elements can be added to crucial pages. It is, in every sense, an inevitable element of the interaction design process.

The focus of a Wireframe is to give an early understanding of a visual page in a project to attain project team and stakeholder approval before the creative phase begins to set off. You will also be able to use a Wireframe to create the global and secondary navigation to make sure the terminology and structure used for the site attain the user's expectations.

It is to be noted that the people more benefit from wireframing are interaction designers, UX designers, Illustrators, Graphic designers, developers, business analysts, stakeholders, Usability ExpertsProject managers, executives, Partners, clients, and others.

You can review and amend the structure of the key pages in a Wireframe format quickly. Iterating all the progress of the Wireframes to a final version will give the design team and client the confidence that the page convincingly accommodates user preferences and requirements while fulfilling the critical project and business objectives.

Wireframes can be used at the onset of the design phase, even though it's used to complete the User-Centered Design process. To get user feedback before the creative process, a prototype usability test can test the Wireframe pages.

It has often been used to make an on-screen delivery using software like Microsoft's Visio, even though it can be hand-drawn simply. It is most convenient to create them in HTML if you use a Wireframe for a prototype usability test.

What makes wireframing more convenient is that you will be able to review with your client in Wireframe as it provides an early visual. Users will also be provided to check it as an early feedback mechanism for prototype usability tests. It is not just a convenient to amend than concept design, and the designer will get absolute confidence once the client and the users approve.

From a practical perspective, the Wireframes can ensure you position the page content and functionality correctly as per the business and the user's needs. This can be used as a good dialogue between members of the project team to agree on the project scope and vision as the project takes its course.

Wireframes can connect fundamental conceptual structures with the visual design of a site or app screen. Wireframes can be classified into the following three:

1. **Low fidelity:** This kind of Wireframe always begins as a simple static outline on paper or a digital canvas. Low-fi Wireframes let you guide the brainstorming

process as developers and designers delineate the main workflows and functions an application might require. They are pretty simple to revise and build on as the team fleshes out ideas as low fidelity is quick outlines. If the group decides to go in a different direction, they haven't wasted valuable resources to build out that idea yet.

2. **Mid fidelity:** More component details can be shown in these Wireframes. It focused on overall page structure and content layout.

3. **High fidelity:** High-fidelity (hi-fi) Wireframes go a step further than low-fi Wireframes to include more details and illustrate simple interactions. Unlike low-fi Wireframes, hi-fi Wireframes are usually clickable and demo fundamental interactions and application flow, like logging in or simple navigations.

4. **Mid fidelity:** More component details can be shown in these Wireframes. It focused on overall page structure and content layout.

5. **High fidelity:** High-fidelity (h-fi) Wireframes go a step further than low-fi Wireframes to include more details and illustrate simple interactions. Unlike low-fi Wireframes, hi-fi Wireframes are usually clickable and demo fundamental interactions and application flow, like logging in or simple navigations.

Wireframes in digital design have another UX artifact and deliverable: the wire flow. It is a combination of Wireframes and flowcharts, two artifacts that UX designers have converged into one for a purpose: to demonstrate and follow interactions that represent task flows in a product such as a web app.

Communicating the user journey is what designers encounter with Wireframes. Wireframe map makes user journey smoothen even though there are enough complex ways of showing user journey.

A Wireframe map combines Wireframes with user journeys (or user flows) to demonstrate the user's journey through a product using Wireframes.

DISADVANTAGES OF WIREFRAMING

It is always challenging for the client to grasp the concept as the Wireframes do not include any design or account for technical implications. Designers need to translate the Wireframes into a design, so communication to support the Wireframe is often required to elaborate why page elements are placed as they are. When content is added, it might be initially difficult to fit within the Wireframe layout, so the copywriter and designer have to work closely to make this fit.

We also learned about the very distinction between Wireframe and Mockup. A Mockup comes to post a Wireframe in the design process, and it builds upon the design of the Wireframe. Mockups certainly are more robust and closer to a fine product than a Wireframe.

There is some kind of differences that can offer you keep Wireframes and Mockups straight:

- Wireframes are black and white, but Mockups are in color.

- When Wireframes are used for functionality, Mockups are used for visuals.

- Wireframes exhibit simply elements of a page; Mockups give substance.

An analogy for both is like the Wireframe represents the blueprint of a house. In two dimensions and black and white, it exhibits the house's layout and how the rooms interconnect.

If a Wireframe is a blueprint, then a Mockup is a two-dimensional rendering of a standing home. It exhibits the style of trim and color of the siding. It provides a cross-section of the living room, finished with wallpaper and granite for the fireplace.

These images can speedily be altered to show different types of wallpaper or a darker wood floor. In the same way, a Mockup can manifest stakeholders' variety of visual looks to a page without altering its structure.

In Chapter 2, we analyzed tools to generate brilliant Mockups. One of the tools we discussed in Chapter 2 is Adobe XD. It is a vector-based UI and UX design tool, and it is possible to design anything from smartphone apps to full-blown websites. We are now aware of what it provides to designers and why it's become a powerful tool in the web design industry. Adobe XD was first launched as "Project Comet" back in 2015 at the annual Adobe MAX conference. Back then, it provided a breath of fresh air to anyone still using Photoshop or Illustrator for their same UI design. Not only that, the web introduces very different design challenges to print.

Those who started out designing websites in Photoshop are aware of the struggles, importantly were responsive, and fluid design is considered. But XD is an entirely different thing. It was created from the ground up, especially with UI and UX design in its mind. It has several features that we have discussed that are never available in other graphics applications.

One of the significant contentions often faced by industry giants like Adobe is a dinosaur with less capacity to be as competent as its younger competitors. Anyhow, a company like Adobe has the resources to evolve and grow spectacularly and the financial stability that would eventually make mastering Adobe XD a good investment. This is what makes it a huge advantage, making Adobe XD very important and potentially the leading UX design tool for the days to come.

Those familiar with digital designing may have used an Adobe application and are somewhat acquainted with the general interface: tool panel on the left, the main area in the center, layers, etc., on the right. The attraction of Adobe XD is that you will feel comfortable as soon as you start using it. The learning curve is slight and occurs primarily around more complex design systems and Symbol overrides.

Adobe XD also can handle complex design systems and Symbol libraries. Moreover, it features intuitive tools for smoothly connecting screens and creating interactive prototypes that can be used in user testing without any code. The recent release of auto-animate allows Prototyping rich interactions even simpler by automatically animating micro-interactions all over the artboards in Adobe XD.

One of its most vital selling points is having an Adobe XD in the Abode ecosystem because chances are you already have Creative Cloud or use other Adobe products weekly. From vectors to photos, the suite of Adobe products has a dedicated tool for most designer needs that will work pretty smoothly with Adobe XD.

To use the software, you have to be aware of Adobe XD's minimum system requirements.

If Mac is your OS, you'll be required to be running Mac OS X or 10.11 and later versions.

Can it possible to work Adobe XD on a non-retina display? Yeah, of course, but it's highly suited that you have to use it on a retina display to avail XD's on-point interface.

Adobe XD can only run on Windows 10 (Anniversary Update) or later, if your tool of choice is Windows (Windows 7 and XP users, no way, sorry.)

Additionally, Adobe XD is available in German, Japanese, English, French, and Korean.

Even though Adobe XD is updated regularly (like every month since its beta version), it is sure to run into some issues.

Most common bugs to watch out for:

When you are using XD, you may face frequent freezes and crashes, resulting in unsaved projects.

The mysterious Error 44, where you may end up in trouble uploading your prototypes in the app. This is the result of a slow network connection, or it may be that you somehow got disconnected while sharing your prototype.

There is a possibility of a bug when panning across your design with the space bar in your Windows 10.

Here are some other minor issues:

- Some keyboard hotkeys not working.

- Changes to stroke and shadow elements while using the Repeat Grid.

- Sometimes, when importing files from Illustrator, there's a bug with the style properties not rendering correctly.

However, if you do run into any of these issues, the good news is that Adobe XD has its feedback platform where you can report bugs and crashes (and make feature requests).

So far, the Adobe XD community is actively posting feedback and bugs, and the XD developers are busy responding and filing these issues. So, hopefully, they will make it on the roadmap to make future updates even more reliable.

Another tool we discussed in this chapter is Mockplus. We have learned that it is a rapid Prototyping tool that helps us to simplify complexity on UI design. It is a desktop-based software tool that supports software Prototyping on multiple major platforms, such as mobile-based, desktop-based, and website-based applications. Pre-built widgets and components are available. In addition, it lets us customize widgets, features, and templates, export HTML & PNG files, and print prototype pages. Prototypes can be previewed by scanning QR codes.

With the help of drag-and-drop WYSIWYG edit, Mockplus will create interactive linking between pages and components. It also supports rapid interactive Prototyping in minutes with a simple interface to design prototypes/Mockups; no coding experience is required. It is also an all-in-one web-based product design platform that provides:

- H-fi interactive Prototyping.
- Simple developer handoff.

- Real-time collaboration.

- Scalable yet reusable design systems.

Your entire product design workflow can be connected into one place. The more exciting part of this is its capability of bringing all participants like developers, designers, product managers, clients, stakeholders, and other design participants for designing faster and collaborating better on the same page.

We can start designing quickly using Mockplus's built-in online Prototyping tool, as there are several ready-to-use icons, UI components, and templates. Animations, interaction transitions, responsive layouts, real-time co-editing like innovative vector tools will help you create mobile app prototypes or websites that work like the real thing.

If you need to import existing designs from any kind of design tools (like Adobe XD, Photoshop, Figma, Axure, and Sketch) to proceed on your design workflow, collaborate with your team, review and leave comments on the screen and transfer all design specs, code snippets, assets, and other deliverables to developers only by a simple link.

Mockplus lets product managers and designers work comfortably online, as its ability to ultimately reduce the gap between designers and developers. A much better explanation is possible though quickly writing or importing a PRD online and referring to the documents and other related design pages collectively. It also helps you with the help of drag and drop to overview all pages of a project in one place and create a user flowchart based on the project pages.

Your entire team will gather and maintain a unified design system is another feature of Mockplus. Import components, fonts, icons, colors, and other assets from design tools like Sketch.

It can be reused instantly from anywhere by other team members at any time.

Even though it is a new player in the Prototyping field, Mockplus has emerged as a real stand-out thus far with a competent team from the orient supported. Instead of overemphasizing functionalities, this agile design tool does give UX the highest priority, making sure anyone of every level can prototype faster, smarter, and more accessible. Its user-centric interaction and highly intuitive interface have gained an increasing number of global customers. If you want to check your app Mockup for free, then you must use the Mockplus app. This tool offers its users 300-plus tools to design swiftly and efficiently.

- Supports interactive prototype.

- Designers, developers, and Managers can collaborate easily.

- Dynamic and reusable design systems.

- Share, Manage, and Maintain with ease.

Mockplus is a one-stop online design platform that helps you to do everything from Prototyping to developer hand-off. Turn your ideas into testable and deliverable designs in one place.

A whole number of valuable components are already built-in Mockplus. Things like image carousels pop up, and scroll boxes will allow your prototype to be interactive from the onset.

Assembling it using their simple drag-and-drop interface is one of its exciting parts as there is no code here.

In terms of its built-in assets, version 2.19 (Pro) significantly evolved. It will introduce nearly 3,000 icons from its earlier 400. All newly introduced icons will be in vector format to be sharp at any size and font. Whatever you need is placed in one place, so you no longer need to search around for icons to use in your project.

The time-saving Auto Recovery feature is one of the new features. You can create interactive commands based on things like page loading and user clicks by using Mockplus.

You can restore the original interaction once the first interaction occurs with the help of Auto Recovery. It requires just a couple of mouse clicks, so you don't need to invest maximum time by tirelessly doing copy and paste.

- **More Impressive Features of Mockplus:** The spirit of the Mockplus team is supplying the best services on Prototyping elaborate ideas with a simple tool. That's the concept of simplism. The desktop Mockplus displays a simple interface formed by three main parts: component and widget library, working space, and project panel. Despite such a concise and clear layout structure, Mockplus is more powerful than it can be imagined. No specialized knowledge on coding and programming is required; users can efficiently and effectively create application Prototyping. Moreover, it does not take too much time to learn the usage of this simple tool. Rather than wasting unnecessary time on tool learning, generating more wonderful and ingenious ideas is better.

Mockplus Pro offers almost 200 pre-designed components that let you work even faster and easier. Rich details offer users extensive choices for their design work, which can be a good reason for labor-saving. Besides, the 400+ icons (with even more coming soon) are enough to help create prototypes.

There are two styles for users to choose when opening Mockplus, Sketch, and Wireframe. Designers can work in any manner you prefer. Some enjoy the Sketch or hand-drawn style because that adds to the authenticity of the Prototyping.

- **Online Designing and Prototyping:** With the help of ready-made components, icons, and templates with Mockplus, we can create a lifelike prototype.

  You can create custom logos, images, components, and illustrations using vector tools. If you want to customize elements with advanced style editing modes, it is also possible. For making a realistic prototype, create different animations, interactions, and transitions with its drag-and-drop functionality and build a rich page or component states. Collaboration is not challenging as we can co-edit the designs team you are working with in real time.

- **Design Collaboration:** One of the most stunning features of Mockplus is its ability to avoid time-consuming by reviewing designs continuously with your team and leaving a comment directly on screens. You will create and manage design tasks to have a complete hand in your design and review process. The PRDs that you created online are also connected with related design pages. Mockplus will help you to manage teams and projects with more accessible roles. If you want to keep track of your team and project activities, the Auto-notifications option will help you to monitor.

- **Design Handoff:** You will be able to design right from Photoshop, Sketch, Adobe XD, Figma, and Axure. You can then transfer designs to developers with auto specs, code snippets, assets, and many more. To start coding quickly, you can download all assets and code snippets in one click.

- **Design System:** Mockplus allows you to gather and manage the design system with your team online. Integrate with design tools like Sketch to import colors, components, fonts, and more. You can share and reuse design assets across your team and link projects and design systems for fast coding. UX designers or researchers always keep looking for new technologies, even though some people go vanilla and create a prototype by hand using paper and pen. Designers are not in a mood to use the sophisticated tool to make it a more accessible alternative. These are some highlighted features of Mockplus that will help your design process to the new horizon with minimum effort.

- **Fully Visualized Interaction:** Interaction design relies on creating an engaging interface with well-planned behaviors. It is drag and drop based at Mockplus, which helps you build interactive prototypes in a completely visualized way, with no repetitive selection or calculation needed.

The Link Point on each component sets up interactive features, and a link between pages, in-page, or cross-page is not a problem.

If we need to make a movable picture when the "Adjust" button is clicked, just click on the button component and drag the link to the required image. Once you have completed it, a dialog window will pop up on the screen to prompt you to define a command for your component.

- **Ready-Made Components:** Pre-designed and readily available components will minimize the overall design time and considerably enhance quality. There are over 200 ready-made components specifically curated to fit both web and mobile apps in Mockplus, making the interactive design less time-consuming. The newly added components contain an image carousel, stack panel, scroll box, popup panel, sliding drawer, and more.

For example, you can attain scrolling for a web prototype by simple drag and drop in the scroll box. Another enhanced way to set scrolling for a mobile prototype with header and footer area fixed.

Cons

Interaction Components

Even though Mockplus is very rapid and straightforward at creating prototypes, but comparatively speaking, it is a little bit weak than other prototypes/Wireframe tool providers at interaction support. To achieve dynamic actions on the current Mockplus 2.0 version needs several steps to do.

However, fortunately, the Mockplus team is well-known for agile development. In the 2.1 version, Mockplus endows outstanding interaction features which are straightforward to use. Create interactive prototypes by defining interactions in the Params Panel to set triggers, and add Target and Commands. Various interaction modes you can choose freely to realize the effect of what you intended. If you want to execute simultaneous actions, that is no problem, and you only need to know it with a single interaction. The practical interaction feature is very brilliant. Moreover, video tutorials and text tutorials about how to use the exchange feature both are available.

- **Devices Supported:**
  - Windows
  - Android
  - iPhone/iPad
  - Mac
  - Web-based
  - Windows mobile
- **Deployment:**
  - Cloud hosted
  - On-premise
- **Language Support:**
  - English
  - Chinese

- **Pricing Model:**
  - Monthly payment
  - One-time payment
  - Annual subscription
- **Customer Types:**
  - Small business
  - Large enterprises
  - Medium business
  - Freelancers

Another tool we discussed in Chapter 2 is Moqups. It is a cloud-based visual collaboration software to help organizations create and validate functional prototypes for designing applications and websites. Teams can utilize whiteboard functionality to collaborate on diagrams, Wireframes, and Mockups. The diagramming tools let designers develop sitemaps, storyboards, or flowcharts and cross-navigate among the components. It is another kind of creative collaboration tool that relies on wireframing but can also be used for Prototyping. It is mainly web-based and is used to make Wireframes for mobile and web applications.

The main difference of Moqups is its fidelity to the Wireframes. Moqups render you full-color stencils and kits for mobile app and web design, including Android, iOS, and Bootstrap.

Moqups distinguishes itself from others in different ways. The software allows for page management and finite object editing, providing designers the freedom to define "master" objects, which will help time-saving when making required changes to the Wireframes during the iteration process.

Let's take an example of creating a master button object with a specific shape, size, and color. This button can be used multiple times throughout the Wireframe. In the iteration process, if you need to change the button's color, instead of changing every single button object, they can change it once, and all the child button objects are subsequently affected.

Moqups offers stencil kits, which let users create personalized designs using multiple elements like icons, fonts, shapes, and widgets from a built-in library. Features include roles and permissions management, activity audit logs, private projects, single sign-on (SSO), multiple teams, and more. Managers can include annotations or comments, modify designs, and communicate via chat, facilitating real-time engagement across projects.

Editing capabilities in Moqups lets users resize, align or rotate objects, bulk edit, rename or lock elements, and adjust specifications using grids, custom guides, rulers, and other alignment tools. It allows integration with different third-party applications, including Google Drive, Slack, and Dropbox.

It is also a visual collaboration program with many tools like design features, whiteboards, and diagrams.

If any companies want to plan, communicate, collaborate, and strengthen people and work management, it's one of the most suitable options.

If you want to create a different visual product to support all sorts of projects, Moqups will help you tremendously. It provides prototypes, Mockups, dashboards, mind maps, Wireframes, and many other ways to echo an organization's message.

It is best suited for executives, corporations, UX professionals, technology-based companies, cross-functional teams, marketing and management agencies, and multiple organizations that work on complicated projects. It also helps companies streamline their processes and track progress. For making better team collaboration and enhanced team communication, Moqups added various fascinating features.

A robust kind of design should have powerful Prototyping, Mockups, and wireframing. You inevitably pictorial your theories, concepts, mission, and vision to make a meaningful impact.

This platform replicates designs and brings them to life with the assistance of different workflows, work charts, and user journeys beforehand.

The information you provide will undoubtedly have a more significant impact on Moqups, with maximum user engagement and productive team collaboration and communication with just one click.

This web design-based tool helps you build all sorts of Mockups, prototypes, and Wireframes for your business. You can make your design more visually appealing and detailed and also navigate between projects and team members.

Another credible choice with flexible drag-and-drop UI, Moqups, is famous as a wireframing tool for interaction design flows. Developers can place icons and images from its built-in library and personal folders into projects. A unique Diagram tool in Moqups lets users make logical markups on the Wireframe to identify where links and interactions will live or even how the UX logic will flow within the app design.

Moqups provide multiple-platform integration like Android, iOS, web, macOS, and Windows. Stencil kits, a range of stylish fonts, organized pages and make Moqups a developer's preferred tool. Moqups's cloud integration lets developers work remotely through Slack, Google Drive, and Dropbox.

KEY FEATURES OF MOQUPS

- An ecosystem of different tools.

- Moqups give you diagrams, Wireframes, prototypes, images, fonts, stencils, icons, and others. It is not required to change one platform to use different features like page management, constructing images, or object editing.

- This kind of streamlined experience helps your work quicker, easier, and more straightforward.

- Flexible, scalable, and powerful features.

The features provided by Moqups features are flexible, scalable, and robust. They enhance as your business develops. You will be able to handle projects of any size and length; its drag-and-drop builder is advanced, and navigation is not complicated with the help of this platform.

- Editing and creating graphics/images from scratch are precise, fast, intuitive, and loaded with dynamic tools.

- Built-in library with graphics and fonts.

- Thousands of icon sets are attached to the built-in library.

- Ready-to-use stencils designed for widespread use cases and custom stencil kits for Android and iOS mobile app design are available.

- Resize, align, style, or rotate objects. You will also be able to group, bulk-edit, lock, and rename elements. With the help of custom guides, rulers, and grids, precise adjustments can be made.

You can choose hundreds of fonts from the integrated Google Font. Advanced controls allow you to tweak the text to match your designs.

MOQUPS DISADVANTAGES

- By not sending renewal notifications of the tool, it creates a kind of obstruction. They deduct the cost post the trial period, and refunds are hard to claim.

- The time-consuming factor is its incapability to select all instead of one-by-one elements and edit it with the drag-and-drop editor. Rearranging flowcharts can be the steadiest process.

- For downloading the Mockup, you need to upgrade to the paid plan. These kinds of things obstruct the purpose of having a free plan.

Resources and Blogs

The platform itself has materials and resources that are more useful than you can think. Moqups also includes informative articles on topics like the difference between low- and hi-fi Wireframes, introducing the multiple teams feature, stick and stack containers, the usage, project folders, live chats in Moqups, etc.

Moqups share with you all about the platform. No requirement for a subscription or creating an account for it.

Extensions, Add-Ons, and Integrations

Moqups has a chrome extension to grab screenshots, use a color selection tool, and create projects. You can also save the screenshots directly to your device and make a mood board.

This program was introduced with a Firefox add-on. It provides the same features like the chrome version, enabling eyedroppers, taking screenshots, and seamlessly creating projects.

Last but not least, Moqups has a fantastic set of integrations that allow you to connect to different platforms and make your work quicker, easier, and simpler.

These integrations included Confluence server, Jira Cloud, Confluence Cloud, Jira server, Dropbox, Slack, Google Drive, and many others. All these have their benefits and up your design game with sharper response time and overall excellence.

Steps that will show you the apps and integrations tab on the Moqups platform are:

- You have to click on the account menu in the top right corner of the app's toolbar, then select account settings and open the accounts setting window in the platform's dashboard. You need to choose the apps and notifications tab.

- Then you will get all the available integrations in just one click.

Support

Moqups has a unique support group that is always available for you. You just need to enter your issue into their specific form for any complaints, and they will respond to you promptly. You can add pictures of your problem as well. All in all, their support executives are customer-friendly and will assist you in using the platform.

Moqups Pricing Plans

The Moqups platform was introduced with a free plan and two paid options. The free plan provides you with essential features and does not ask you to enter your payment card or obligations. This opportunity provides you with enough time to venture into the parts and make up your mind if you want to use them further. The paid plans come with outstanding features that help you enhance your collaboration and communication.

The free plan only has one project, which is constrained to 200 objects and 5MB of storage.

Another tool we discussed in this chapter is Mockplus iDoc. We have a whole lot of tools that help make communication as convenient as possible for all parties. One of these magic tools to support this possibility is Mockplus iDoc—a robust product design collaboration tool for designers and developers by creating a connected online space for product teams. Designers can export their designs from Adobe, Sketch, and Photoshop, and the tool will certainly prepare all the assets, specifications, and code snippets you require.

To make a robust online design collaboration solution for designers and developers, Mockplus introduced Mockplus iDoc, a new brand product design collaboration tool, on November 8, 2020.

Mockplus iDoc is a vital product design collaboration tool for developers and designers. It provides a connected online space for product collaborators. It is not just design workflow but also allows teams with the design handoff. It highly facilitates the handoff by taking designs from Sketch, Photoshop, and Adobe XD and exporting them into a format that will help team members generate style guides, code snippets, specs, and assets.

Designers will be able to hand off designs with accurate specs, code snippets, assets, and interactive prototypes automatically with the help of Mockplus iDoc.

It is the ultimate online design collaboration tool between developers and designers. All kinds of product design workflow, from design to development, can be connected, and your entire team can focus on building outstanding products together.

Mockplus iDoc is a popular all-in-one online design collaboration tool that lets developers, designers, and product managers import, prototype, test, share, and handoff web/app designers with automatic specs, code snippets, assets.

The product team can easily import designs from Sketch/PS/XD, create UI flows and interactive prototypes, check and download design assets/specs/code snippets, upload and preview files from Axure/JustinMind/Mockplus/Office/Excel, handoff designs, and manage team members with ease.

One of the reasons you should choose Mockplus iDoc is its ability for online design collaboration and handoff tool for designers, developers, and product managers to upload, prototype, comment, test, share, and handoff designs with automaticity specs, assets, and code snippets.

Here are key features of Mockplus iDoc:

- Import designs with automatic specs, assets, and code snippets from Sketch, XD, and PS.

- Create UI flow and interactive prototypes with drag and drop.

- Comment, review, test, and iterate designs with simple clicks.

- Check, copy, and download design specs, assets, and code snippets with one click.

- Upload prototypes from Justinmind/Axure/Mockplus and documents.

- You can make a Handoff design with accurate specs, code snippets, and assets with just a click.

It will not be a mountainous claim if we say that Mockplus iDoc is ahead of any other similar tools you've ever accustomed. Take a deep to find out what makes it unique.

- **Various Ways of Accessing Specs:** iDoc provides three specs modes. You can maintain any layers; single or multiple layers also can be selected; and you can hold down Alt to convert specs to percentage values.

New Features of Mockplus iDoc

Gesture Interaction

You will have more choices rather than the simple click and jump triggering mode. Mockplus iDoc provides a different kinds of gesture interactions:

Doubleclick, OnLoad, Press, and Swipe up/down/left/right. These productive gesture interactions make prototype demos more practical.

Cons

- The prototype will be slow when it is tested on mobile.
- The Mockup needed to be permanently downloaded from the Internet.
- The logo of Mockplus will pop up when previewing the prototype.

In Chapter 3, we detailed different kinds of Wireframe tools.

Designers can quickly and effectively mock up an outline of a design through Wireframe tools.

You can drag-and-drop placeholders for headers, images, and content and quickly move them around to create a first draft that can be iterated on later.

Technically speaking, You don't require a comprehensive Wireframe tool—a flowchart app is enough. But Wireframe tools outstanding functionalities will be much helpful for a website designer.

These include:

- **An Uploadable or In-Built UI Kit:** Basically, you have to select a Wireframe app. It will have an in-built UI component library or help you to upload your own to it.

- **Scalable Mockup Fidelity:** Good Wireframe apps will allow you the free hand to scale between a stunning basic gray-scale low-fi Mockup and more graphically complex hi-fi Mockups.

- **Collaborative Working:** It is possible to share work digitally and let others make changes or leave feedback. It is an essential function in any Wireframe tool.

- **Export Options:** Basically, you need to export sections of it as HTML or get access to basic CSS code once you've completed your Mockup so you can implement development more rapidly.

One of the tools we discussed in this chapter is Sketch. It is a vector-based tool used for mobile and desktop UI design, prototypes, and Mockups, and it has become an industry standard. This outstanding tool lets you edit and manipulate photos.

If you are a novice and have not seen a sketch before, that doesn't hold you back from using Sketch as it is profoundly user-friendly and will allow you to learn so quickly. It's solely for designers who want to cherish, not the layman cup of tea, and is suitable for teams providing client needs. It's intended for Mac users as its Mac-only app.

As a renowned design tool for UX/UI designers, Sketch allowed a platform for Prototyping, vector editing, and collaboration. It included a growing library of hundreds of plugins that extend its functionality.

Wireframing in Sketch is almost the same as Adobe XD as it provides template/skits and drawing tools. You will be able to use Symbols excessively, which are reusable components. This can be defined once and used a lot of times (buttons, etc.). Instantiated Symbols can take on any changes made to the "master" Symbol. You inevitably have to make considerable changes throughout the wireframing process. So it will be one of the most valuable things to be mentioned.

Designers can create hi-fi Wireframes, Mockups, and Mockups. It is not a cloud-based app, and one of the main problems is that it only works with macOS.

Sketch has become one of the top vector graphics editors among designers in recent years.

As a Mac-only vector design program, its focus is on creating interactive app and web designs prototypes. Sketch's outstanding design working model enthuses your clients as it will provide an excellent feel for how everything looks and responds. That will help them give more practical feedback on the functionality (UI) and UX. So it lets informed approval in advance of the development stage, which will minimize any contentions that will save time and money.

Sketch mainly focused on collaborative design for screens, and it's relatively new to the fray. Other UX designs like Adobe XD (XD stands for Experience Design), introduced in 2016 as part of Adobe's Creative Cloud for Windows and Mac. It is also a vector-based tool.

A second vector-based competitor is Studio from the heavyweight design system management platform, InVision. It has a built-in advanced animation module that is not available in Sketch and XD. The InVision platform lets you sync your work done in Sketch using their Craft Manager plugin.

Sketch provides multiple subscription models, costing $99 per year per device (either a mobile or computer), for individuals. This year of updates is also included in this model and Sketch Cloud (for online sharing and collaborating). You can renew for $69 per year to regain cloud benefits and regular updates. Getting volume licensing ranges from $64 per year per device for two to nine devices down to $49 each for 50 or more devices.

It would be mentioned that you will get only a single seat (for use on one computer only) when you purchase a license; you have to buy two seats if you are going to use multiple Macs, like a laptop and desktop. Many subscription-based apps often let two seats per license as a friendly act for hard-working creatives who work on their desktop at the office and on their laptops at home. A related inconvenience is that if you want to use Sketch on a new Mac or if you've had to reformat your drive, you need to unregister Sketch from your old machine/drive and then re-register.

BENEFITS OF SKETCH

- You can learn it quickly as it's a straightforward, intuitive interface.

- You will be able to create designs for multiple devices.

- If a client interacts with a laptop, desktop, phone, or tablet design, she can preview what would happen.

- Sketch Cloud syncing and sharing are helpful collaboration features.

- A collection of plugins can be used with Sketch (Craft, Abstract, Flinto, etc.).

- The toolbar is similar to Mac.

- Affordable.

When it comes to the benefits of Sketch, you can compare it with Photoshop. For example, you will work similarly to

Photoshop, but it only consumes a lower price and can save your disk space.

As a leading Prototyping tool, Sketch has the instinct even to overtake photoshop at some point. The sketch is much apt at screen design than Photoshop because it was explicitly designed for a new, more modern, purpose-built tool.

Sketch Basic Features

- Drawing, shape, and text tools.

- Edit shape points and Bezier curves.

- Arrangement operations (alignment, bring to front, distribution).

- Boolean tools (union, subtract, intersect, difference).

- The Sketch is meant for Prototyping, not for drawing.

Define hotspots: You can also assign areas of the screen as scrolling/non-scrolling and link and cross-link sections, instances, menus, pages, and Symbols. It is also possible to import text or images to populate the prototype with more realistic data than placeholders. If you are looking for designing with high-level precision, Sketch is spectacularly useful.

- It will provide tools for high precision (grids and pixels grid, Smart Guides, rulers, etc.).

- Smart Guides will pop up before you set off your drawing for optimal precision.

- Holding "Alt" will help you to show the distance between the selected layer and others, as well as between the coating and the artboard.

- Choose two layers and place them together.

- The Distribute Objects option helps you minimize distances between layers.

- You can set your layout grid.

- More Great Sketch Features

- With the scale tool, you can scale every property—radius, border, shadow/inner shadow, and size.

- Pixel fitting helps you retain sharp pixels as you resize or align shapes.

- And colors are placed based on how often they're used as there is automatic detection of colors in your document.

- The color tool will help you to store your palette for a single document or globally.

- If you want more control over your colors, you can change RGB to HSB.

- Gradients are helpful for buttons, backgrounds, and icons.

- Use angular gradients for circular backgrounds and radial gradients for extensive backgrounds.

- You can make a customizable background blur; all layers underneath the one selected will blur automatically.

- Text Styles allow you to reuse your preferred typography style across layers (set a global style).

- You can create reusable elements or Symbols to share across artboards; it will sync all the others if you are updated one (if another team member updates a Symbol, you can approve the update or detach it from your library).

- You will be able to migrate from a library filled with icons and logos in Photoshop or Illustrator to Sketch.

- Auto-Save option will save your changes so you can work comfortably.

- The version history of your design also created by Auto-Save.

- You have to work on an infinite canvas if you are first starting in Sketch. You will be able to customize the toolbar by right-clicking and setting your favorites by dragging.

A screen or an interaction within a screen is what an artboard demonstrates in Sketch. When creating an artboard, you can select from a list of standard screen sizes for iOS, Android, print, and web. It is pretty amusing that you are free to customize your own. An Artboard Manager plugin for OCD-level organization is also provided—you can snap your artboards into columns and rows to neaten them up.

A different kind of resolution or platform is represented in Pages in Sketch. You have to pull them all into a Page if you are going to create an artboard for iOS, and then you will be able to create another page for your Android design.

A Sketch file can hold multiple pages and artboards. This helps you to access your workflow easily.

Clicking on a layer helps you open up an inspector to the right, where you can change properties like most screen design tools.

Simplicity is what defines a tool like Sketch. It's pretty amusing just how simple it is to navigate, even as a newcomer.

It would be inconvenient to use photoshop tools for straightforward design jobs, so you can use something like Sketch as it saves your time and stress, and money.

Its outstanding ability to reuse elements with ease, again and again, will help you save your time as a designer.

Sketch's layout and vector drawing are robust and straightforward, so it's quite a pleasure to dive into it—even if you have too much more time experimenting.

The Sketch isn't a standalone app that requires extensive procedures to bring all your work together either; it facilitates almost seamless integration with the likes of Framer, Principle, and Marvel, which rarely leaves you wanting.

It's a wonder that Sketch is so cheap at a one-off payment of $99 (including free updates for a year).

A sketch can be downloaded from the company's site (sketchapp.com); it will provide a 30-day free trial, which can be used with no credit card.

It is a fact that MacOS 10.13.4 (High Sierra) or later version is only suitable for Sketch.

More powerful, RAM-loaded Macs are suitable if you use complex, multipage documents with hundreds of artboards.

Right on the download page, you will get Beginner's Guide, tutorials and tips, extensive documentation, and links to its social media and developer communities, chats, and blog, and

Dribbble. It's pretty scintillating that you would see a list of global design community events and meet-ups. Additionally, the site provides several free and premium Sketch App UX/UI resources, including mobile UI kits, Wireframe kits, Mockups, dashboards, templates, icons, and concepts.

Cons

- It is pretty buggy … even the latest v47.1 can be frustratingly so.

- Unexpected crashes and malfunctions of the app and supported plugins.

- It's Mac-only (sorry, PC users).

- The photo-editing capabilities are limited.

- Difficult to use with a Wacom tablet.

Another tool we discussed in Chapter 3 is Figma. It has become a revolutionary graphics editing apps that transformed the design world profoundly. The better part of Figma is the fact that it's free to use. Figma was co-founded by Dylan Field in 2013 and got a $14 million Series A back in 2015. Dylan states that Figma wants to "do what Google Docs did for interface design for text editing in a TechCrunch article."

It is one of the web-based graphics editing and UI design app. You will be able to do all sorts of graphic design work, from designing mobile app interfaces, wireframing websites, Prototyping designs, crafting social media posts, and everything in between. When it comes to functionality and features, Figma has undoubtfully a close similarity with Sketch.

But of course, its tremendous ability in team collaboration makes Figma distinct from any other such tools. Suppose you are in a profound puzzle about such outstanding capability of Figma. In that case, it's time to clear out all such confusion as we will explain how Figma will enhance your design process and is undoubtfully better than other programs at helping designers and teams work together smoothly.

You can work directly on your browser in Figma, which makes it different from other kinds of graphic editing tools. This will help you to access your projects from any platform or computer. So you can start designing without having to buy different licenses or install the software.

WHY IS WEB-BASED A GOOD THING?

You don't need to download software, install it, and continually update.

Your work will automatically be saved to a shared space in the Cloud, so your files need not be saved or organized.

One URL will be the source of truth that everyone can see. So you don't need to continually upload, sync, and arrange PNGs in multiple places.

Another reason why designers love this app is that Figma offers a generous free plan to create and store three active projects at a time. So it would be a better option for you to learn, experiment, and work on small projects.

- **Figma Works on Any Platform:** Figma can work on any operating system. What you need is a web browser. Figma can be used in Windows PCs, Macs, Linux machines, and even Chromebooks. You can expect only this design tool of its type to make this happen, and in shops that use hardware running multiple operating systems, which help everyone share, open, and edit Figma files.

Designers always use Macs, and developers use Windows PCs in many organizations. To make all of them come together, Figma helps a massive role. It also stops a different kind of PNG-pong (where updated images are bounced back and forth between design team disciplines). You don't need any mediating mechanism in Figma to make design work accessible to everyone.

- **Collaboration Is Simple and Familiar:** Teams will be able to collaborate as Figma is a browser-based tool. You can see a circular avatar on the top of the app to view what others are viewing and editing in a file. Tracking is easy in Figma as each person in the team has a named cursor. You can see what others are viewing at that time.

  By just clicking others' avatar zooms, real-time file collaboration lets you control design drifting. It is defined as either misinterpreting or straying from an agreed-upon design. You might have known that things like design drifting usually happen when an idea is conceived and implemented with much consultation while a project is taking its shape. This will, of course, often put upside down all of your established design, which in turn causes friction and re-work.

  You can see what the team is designing in real time by simply opening a shared file through a design lead in Figma. This feature helps the design lead intervene, correct course, and save many hours that would have otherwise been wasted if a designer misinterpreted the brief or user story. This will not be available in another tool like Sketch.

- **Figma Uses Slack for Team Communication:** Slack is used as a Figma communication channel. Whatever comments or design edits made in Figma are "slacked" to the team if a Figma channel is created in Slack; this functionality is unavoidable when designing live as changes to a Figma file will update every other instance where the file is embedded. It can then avoid potential disturbance. Changes to a Mockup are immediately vetted, even though it's required or not, and the feedback channel is live.

- **Share Easy to Files:** If you use Figma as a web UX designing tool, it will take only a few minutes. You don't need to search through every conversation held with the client, and everything can be solved with just some clicks. This feature would be tremendously helpful if a developer asked to deliver some files to his clients on short notice.

  Figma can get it done in just five minutes, as its a quietly a time-saver, but you need to spend more time using a traditional process.

- **Numerous Plugins Available:** Figma provides several useful plugins, so you don't need to search externally for plugins. Some of the best plugins are Iconify, Unsplash, Blobs Maker, Component Replacer, Remove BG, Content Reel, etc. We named only a few here, which is why web development companies select this software over others in the fast-moving market.

Another tool we discussed in Chapter 3 is UXPin. It is a code-based design tool that merges engineering and design into one unified process. It is possible to build prototypes that feel real because of variables, state-based animations, conditional interactions, and intense expressions. It does mean UXPin will let you prototype anything on the web accurately. This web-based design tool is somewhat different from others that you may have been familiarized with. It is an end-to-end UX platform. It is not merely used for just a screen or page design but focuses on creating design systems.

When other tools focus on User Interaction, UX emphasizes user experience, which helps to create new experiences altogether. It is to be noted that even though a single person can use it, the UXPin material design UI kit will also be used for larger teams of designers.

UXPin lets create designs from the conceptualization stage to testing and development while maintaining design consistency all around. UXPin allows robust and credible understanding between designers, developers, engineers, and other stakeholders involved in the project. It has tremendous ability to enable multiple users to lean in on the work process.

The UXPin UI kit will provide you with several items, interactions, variables, elements, and expressions. The most valuable thing is its ability to transfer the items into HTML code and tangible interaction, which in turn lets you save your precious time. UXPin is secure, fast, and a cross-collaborative tool to create designs for any screen-based digital solution or product.

UXPin will meet all your design needs, no matter whether it is simple or complex digital solutions. This software allows you to leverage specific requirements that require some intricate work.

UXPin provides native desktop apps available for both Windows and macOS devices as well as its web-based version.

MERGE IN UXPin

Users will be able to import and keep in sync coded React.js components from GIT repositories to the UXPin Editor with the help of Merge. The ingredients used by developers during the process of development are identical to the imported parts.

Components will look, feel, and function (interactions, data) like the actual product experienced by the end-users.

Merge designers will use components in the code repository without any extra work or expertise in the coding.

No need for redrawing elements that have already been coded.

They can test advanced use cases with interactions and data available in production code.

Because the components used by the designers have already been coded, engineers can enhance their workflows.

They can use auto-generated specifications for every design that refers to the composed, real JSX.

It is possible to be a part of the advanced Prototyping process by writing custom components, iterating on code, and connecting elements to data sources.

Design ops/design systems teams can build unified design systems serving both engineers and designers from a single source of truth set up in code.

It is essential to control changes to components in the system by controlling properties of React.js components (flow or typescript types prop-types and interfaces).

The version of the design system has to control and required coordinate releases via GitHub for both engineers and designers.

Engineering and design leaders will be able to connect and synchronize engineering and designing processes.

To understand the agile process without a waterfall handoff.

It is crucial to benefit from the shorter path to testing ideas and delivering new products/features to the market.

Supported versions:

- iOS 10 or later

- Android 5.0 or later

You can download the app from App Store or Google Play.

You are allowed to be logged in two devices at a time if you are using UXPin on more than one computer. You can work in the browser from one and one with an open desktop app.

It doesn't make any problem if you are offline, as it will allow you to continue editing the currently open page in the UXPin desktop app. However, you need to remember that some things might not work in such a situation. You need to keep the desktop app and the browser open until the Internet connection is returned, which is when your changes will be synced automatically.

Another tool we discussed in Chapter 3 is Axure RP. It is a robust design tool for creating highly interactive HTML prototypes for mobile, web, and desktop application projects. Rapid Prototyping is the main focus of the tool. Axure RP is an on-premise application development platform that lets users prototype and Wireframe software projects. It helps non-technical businesses to publish diagrams and prototypes in the Cloud or on-premise platforms and demonstrate designs for clients.

Axure RP's features comprise Sketch, Wireframe, flow diagrams, Prototyping, notes, Axure share publishing, co-authoring, revision history, team project hosting, SAML-based SSO, author and reviewer accounts, and workspace access management. The platform's diagramming and documentation tools are used to create and manage flowcharts, Wireframes, Mockups, user journeys, personas, and idea boards. Additionally, Axure RP comes with built-in and custom libraries, which enable users to enhance and style diagrams with fills, gradients, lines, and text formatting.

Axure RP comes with AxShare App for iOS and Android platforms, which provide interactive view possible to types on smartphones and tablets. It is a handy tool, and you will be able to use it for Prototyping, wireframing, and creating specifications, commonly used. Axure RP is always used by business analysts, UX designers, information architects, user researchers, and product managers to websites and design applications. It is possible to quickly prototype, then visually present your website or application without writing a single line of code.

Axure lets users quickly create prototypes and Wireframes from any rough ideas they may have.

WHAT CAN YOU CREATE IN AXURE RP?

It will help you to use it in the Design and Research phases of a project.

Axure is one of the excellent Prototyping tools to date. It provides outstanding features like resizing, drag and drop, and many similar options. You will be able to create highly interactive designs in Axure. Its quite profound choice of rapid Prototyping makes your creativity fast deliverable to the clients. Collaboration between the engineers is also allowed with the help of a quick and shareable portable file format. You will get responsive and adaptive designs. It will provide you with multiple widgets and templates that can be customized according to your wishes and possible to use in another project.

Index

Printed in the United States
by Baker & Taylor Publisher Services